THE BLUE PLAQUES OF LONDON

L.M. Palis

CEN

First published 1989

© L. M. Palis 1989

British Library Cataloguing in Publication Data

Palis, Luis
The blue plaques of London.
1. London. Blue plaques.
I. Title
942.1

ISBN 1-85336-086-4

942.11 (88)

2 5 SEP 1989

Equation is an imprint of the Thorsons Publishing Group, Wellingborough, Northamptonshire NN8 2RQ, England.

Typeset by Harper Phototypesetters Limited, Northampton
Printed in Great Britain by Richard Clay Limited, Bungay, Suffolk

1 3 5 7 9 10 8 6 4 2

CONTENTS

Introductory Note   4

PART 1: People   5

PART 2: Selected Historical Sites   167

Index of People   197

Index of Historical Sites   206

Index of Streets   208

INTRODUCTORY NOTE

'London; a nation, not a city.'

Disraeli, *Lothair*

The truth of Disraeli's words will immediately strike anyone who has taken even the most cursory notice of the many wall plaques and other memorials that adorn public buildings and private houses throughout London. It is a nation, moreover, that has always welcomed immigrants and refugees from almost every country and culture in the world and from every field of human endeavour: novelists, poets, scientists, politicians, social reformers, philosophers, princes and presidents, musicians and composers, artists, scholars, soldiers and sailors, doctors and explorers . . .

This book is a, necessarily selective, guide to the commemorative wall plaques of London — principally the famous blue ceramic circles, but also to a variety of other memorials to the great and the good, the famous and the infamous residents of London's streets and squares. The aim has been to enable the visitor to plan itineraries in advance, or simply to use the book as a handy pocket companion.

The first part of the book contains an alphabetical listing by surname of people whose achievements have led to a commemorative plaque being erected to their memory. In addition to giving the address and, where relevant, the postal district, each entry also contains a concise summary of the subject's life and career.

Part 2 is a select list of historical sites — for instance, City churches destroyed in the Great Fire of London.

Finally, there are three comprehensive indexes to enable the reader to locate individual people, sites, or streets quickly and easily.

A

ABBAS, Ali Mohamed (1922–79)

33 Tavistock Square, WC1

Barrister and one of the founders of Pakistan. Lived here from 1945 to 1979.

ADAMS, Henry Brooks (1838–1918)

98 Portland Place, W1

American historian, born in Boston, Mass., the son of C.F. Adams, US ambassador to the Court of St James, and grandson of John Adams (see next entry), second president of the USA. His *magnum opus* was the *History of the United States during the Administration of Jefferson and*

Madison, published in 9 volumes 1889–91.

ADAMS, John (1735–1826)

9 Grosvenor Square, W1

American statesman, born in Braintree (now Quincy), Mass., the son of a farmer of English descent. Educated at Harvard and admitted to the Boston bar in 1758. Strongly committed to the colonial cause, he was one of the signatories of the Declaration of Independence. Minister to England 1785–8. While in London he wrote his *Defence of the Constitution of the United States* (3 vols., 1787). Became vice-president under Washington and in 1796 was elected second president of the USA. He was defeated in 1800 and retired to Quincy, where he died.

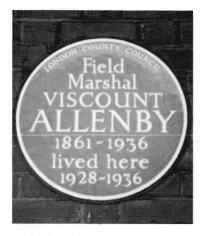

Physician and pioneer in the professional education of women. Born in London and brought up in Aldeburgh, Suffolk. After much opposition she passed the Apothecaries' Hall examination in 1865 to qualify as a doctor, receiving an MD degree from the University of Paris in 1870. She founded the New Hospital for Women, now the Elizabeth Garrett Anderson Hospital, and in 1908 was elected mayor of Aldeburgh, the first woman mayor in England. She was the sister of Dame Millicent Fawcett (see p. 51).

ALLENBY, Edmund Henry Hynman, 1st Viscount (1861–1936)

24 Wetherby Gardens, SW5

British general, educated at Haileybury and Sandhurst. Joined the Inniskilling Dragoons in 1882, took part in the South African war 1899–1902. On the outbreak of the First World War he commanded the 1st Cavalry Division in France and in October 1915 took command of the 3rd Army. Commanded the Egyptian expeditionary force in 1917 and defeated the Turks at Gaza, capturing Jerusalem and, in October 1918, Damascus. A scholarly, methodical soldier, Allenby was raised to the peerage in 1919.

ANDERSON, Elizabeth Garrett (1836–1917)

20 Upper Berkeley Street, W1

ASQUITH, Herbert Henry, 1st Earl of Oxford and Asquith (1852–1928)

20 Cavendish Square, W1

English statesman, born at Morley, Lancashire, the son of a businessman. Educated at Balliol College, Oxford, where he took a First in Classics, called to the bar at

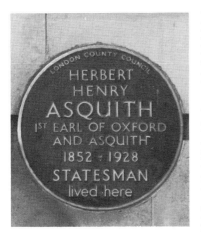

Lincoln's Inn in 1876. His second wife was Margot Tennant. Elected Liberal MP for East Fife in 1886; home secretary 1892–5, chancellor of the Exchequer 1905–8. Succeeded Campbell-Bannerman as prime minister in April 1908. Under Asquith's administration a number of important measures were introduced, including provision for old age pensions and national insurance. England under Asquith also saw suffragette troubles and the outbreak of the First World War.

ATTLEE, Clement Richard, 1st Earl Attlee (1883–1967)

19 Monkhams Avenue, Redbridge

English Labour statesman, born in Putney, educated at Haileybury and University College, Oxford. Called to the bar in 1905, entered Parliament in 1922. Parliamentary secretary to Ramsay MacDonald 1922–4, postmaster-general 1931, deputy prime minister in Churchill's war cabinet 1942–5 and subsequently prime minister. Lived here.

AUSTEN, Jane (1775–1817)

23 Hans Place, SW1

Novelist, born at Steventon, Hampshire, where her father was rector. Began writing early. Her first twenty-five years were spent at Steventon and thereafter she lived in Bath, Southampton, Chawton, and Winchester, where she died. Four of her novels were published anonymously during her lifetime, the other two under her name posthumously: *Sense and Sensibility* (1811), *Pride and Prejudice* (1813), *Mansfield Park* (1814), and *Emma* (1815), and, after her death, *Northanger Abbey* and *Persuasion* (1818). She is buried in Winchester Cathedral.

B

BADEN–POWELL, Robert Stephenson Smyth, 1st Baron (1857–1941)

9 Hyde Park Gate, SW7

British general and founder of the Boy Scouts. Born in London, educated at Charterhouse. Joined the army and saw service in India and Afghanistan. Became a national hero as the defender of Mafeking during the South African war (1899–1900). Founded the Boy Scout movement in 1908 and, with his sister Agnes, the Girl Guides in 1910.

BAGEHOT, Walter (1826–77)

12 Upper Belgrave Street, SW1

Economist, banker, and writer, born at Langport, Somerset. Educated at University College, London, where he graduated in mathematics. Bagehot married the daughter of Sir James Wilson, founder and owner of *The Economist*, and after his father-in-law's death assumed the editorship of the paper. His works include *The English Constitution* (1867), *Physics and Politics* (1872), and *Economic Studies* (1880).

BAIRD, John Logie (1888–1946)

3 Crescent Wood Road, Sydenham, SE26

Scottish television pioneer, born at Helensburgh. Educated at Larchfield Academy and the University of Glasgow. Began developing the

transmission of television images in 1922 and gave his first demonstrations in 1926. His 240-line system was adopted by the BBC in 1929 but was superseded by a rival system in 1937. Baird also developed systems for transmitting three-dimensional and colour images. He died at Bexhill-on-Sea.

132-5 Long Acre, WC2

From this site, Baird broadcast the first television programme in Great Britain on 30 September 1929.

BALDWIN, Stanley, 1st Earl Baldwin of Bewdley (1867–1947)

93 Eaton Square, SW1

British Conservative statesman, born in Bewdley, educated at Harrow and Trinity College, Cambridge. Entered the family iron and steel business and became an MP in 1906. Succeeded Bonar Law as prime minister unexpectedly in 1923. His

premiership saw the General Strike (1926) and the abdication of Edward VIII (1937). He resigned soon after the abdication crisis and was made an earl.

BALLANTYNE, Robert Michael (1825–94)

Mount Park Road, South Harrow

Scottish author of books for boys, the best known of which are *The Coral Island*, *Martin Rattler*, and *The Young Fur Traders*. His autobiographical *Personal Reminiscences in Book-making* was published in 1893. Ballantyne was also a gifted water-colour artist. He died in Rome.

BARBOSA, Ruy (1849–1923)

17 Holland Park Gardens, W14

Brazilian statesman, born in San Salvador. A lawyer by profession, he entered Brazilian politics in the

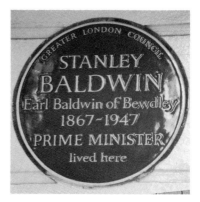

movement to abolish slavery and took an active part in the republican revolution of 1889. He was co-author of the Brazilian Constitution. After the establishment of a military dictatorship he fled to Argentina and then to Britain, where he wrote his famous *Letters from England*. He was appointed to the panel of judges of the Permanent Court of Arbitration of the Hague. He died in Rio de Janeiro.

BARING, Sir Francis (1740–1810)

Manor House Library, Old Road, SE13

Merchant and banker, born in Exeter, lived here 1797–1810.

BARNARDO, Thomas John (1845–1905)

58 Solent House, Ben Jonson Road, E1

Philanthropist and founder of homes for destitute children. Born in Dublin, son of a German immigrant of Spanish descent. Came to London in 1866 to train as a medical missionary and was appalled by the plight of homeless children in the capital. He established a mission for destitute children in the East End in 1867, followed by a number of homes throughout the London area which were later named after him. He died at Surbiton, Surrey.

BARNETT, Dame Henrietta (1851–1936)
BARNETT, Canon Samuel (1844–1913)

Spaniards Road, Heath End, NW3

Dame Henrietta Barnett, founder of Hampstead Garden Suburb, and Samuel Barnett, social reformer, lived here.

BARRY, Sir Charles (1795–1860)

The Elms, Clapham Common (North Side), SW4

Architect, born in London, educated privately. In Italy 1817–20. Designed the Travellers' Club (1831), the Manchester Athenaeum (1836), and the Reform Club (1837). After the old Palace of Westminster was burned down on 16 October 1834 Barry was commissioned to design its replacement. The work was completed after his death by his son Edward Middleton. Barry was knighted in 1852 and died here.

BAZALGETTE, Sir Joseph William (1819–91)

17 Hamilton Terrace, NW8

Born at Enfield, Middlesex. He designed London's main drainage scheme while he was chief engineer for the Metropolitan Commission of Sewers, later replaced by the Metropolitan Board of Works. Other works undertaken for the Board include the Victoria, Albert, and Chelsea Embankments, the new bridges at Putney and Battersea, Northumberland Avenue, and the Woolwich Steam Ferry. He was knighted in 1874 and died at Wimbledon Park.

BEAUFORT, Sir Francis (1774–1857)

51 Manchester Street, W1

British Admiral who after a

distinguished naval career was appointed Hydrographer to the Royal Navy. He invented the 12-degree Beaufort Scale for measuring wind force. First adopted by the British Admiralty in 1838, the Beaufort Scale was adopted by the International Meteorological Committee in 1874.

BEECHAM, Sir Thomas, 2nd Bart (1879–1961)

31 Grove End Road, NW8

Conductor and impresario, son of Sir Joseph Beecham, the pill millionaire. Born in St Helens, Lancashire, educated at Rossall and Wadham College, Oxford. Conductor at the Metropolitan Opera House, New York, 1943; founded the Royal Philharmonic orchestra in 1947. Lived here.

BENES, Edvard (1884–1948)

26 Gwendolen Avenue, SW15

Czech statesman, born in Kozlany,

Bohemia. Educated at the universities of Prague, Paris, and Dijon, where he qualified as a Doctor of Law in 1908. He followed Masaryk in his struggle to liberate the Czechs from Austrian rule; both founded the Czechoslovak National Council. He was Minister of Foreign Affairs of the new Republic, representing his country at the League of Nations. In 1935, after Masaryk's retirement, he was elected president of the Republic, but after Hitler's invasion in 1938 he resigned and went into exile in London. On 16 May 1945, he returned to Prague and was re-elected President, but under pressure from his Communist prime minister, Klements Gottwald, he resigned three years later. He died at Segimovo Usti.

BEN-GURION, David (1886–1973)

75 Warrington Crescent, W9

Jewish statesman, first prime minister of Israel, born at Plonsk in Poland. Emigrated to Palestine in

1906, served in the Jewish Legion, which he had helped raise in America, against the Turks in Palestine. Became leader of the Mapai Party and subsequently took power at the birth of the state of Israel in May 1948. Lived here.

BENNETT, (Enoch) Arnold (1867–1931)

75 Cadogan Square, SW1

Novelist and man of letters, born near Hanley, Staffordshire, the son of a solicitor. Educated locally and at London University. Took up journalism and in 1893 became assistant editor (later editor) of *Woman*. Lived in Paris for eight years from 1900. Bennett was the complete professional writer whose works brought him considerable wealth. They include *The Old Wives' Tale* (1908), *Clayhanger* (1910), and *Hilda Lessways* (1911), all of which are set in the 'Five Towns' of the

Potteries. He was also the author of the popular play *Milestones* (1912), written with Edward Knoblock. He died in Chiltern Court, Baker Street.

BERLIOZ, Hector (1803–69)

58 Queen Anne Street, W1

French composer, born in Côte-Saint-André, Isère, near Grenoble. Studied medicine to begin with but then entered the Paris Conservatoire in 1826. Married the Shakespearean actress Harriet Smithson, who inspired the *Symphonie Fantastique*. For a time Berlioz produced music criticism as well as composing until the success of his symphonic *Harold en Italie* (1834) made him financially independent for a time. He never achieved the reputation in France that he enjoyed elsewhere in Europe, including England. His works include *Grande Messe des Morts* (1837), *Roméo et Juliette* (1838), and *La Damnation de Faust* (1846).

BESANT, Annie (*née* Wood, 1847–1933)

39 Colby Road, SE19

Social reformer and Theosophist, born in London. Married the Revd Frank Besant but separated from him in 1873. A friend of George Bernard Shaw (see p. 134), she joined the Fabian Society (see p. 178) and became closely associated with the Theosophical Society and its high priestess, Madame Blavatsky. In her later years she became a champion of Indian nationalism and died in Madras.

BLAKE, William (1757–1827)

17 South Molton Street, W1

Poet and painter, born in London, the son of a hosier. Apprenticed to the engraver James Basire in 1771 and studied at the Royal Academy school. Married Catherine Boucher in 1782. In 1783 he produced *Poetical Sketches* and this was followed by the famous *Songs of*

Innocence (1789) and in due course the companion work *Songs of Experience* (1794). His mystical and visionary temperament is shown to the full in the prophetic books, such as *The Book of Thel* (1789), *The Marriage of Heaven and Hell* (1791), *The French Revolution* (1791), *The Four Zoas* (originally called *Vala*, 1797), *Milton* and *Jerusalem* (begun in 1804), though he is perhaps best remembered for some of his lyric pieces, such as 'The Tiger'. Apart from illustrating his own work Blake also devised startlingly original illustrations for Young's *Night Thoughts*, Blair's *The Grave*, and for the book of Job. His friends and disciples included the sculptor John Flaxman (see p. 52) and the painter Samuel Palmer.

8 Marshall Street, W1

Blake was born in a house on this site 28 November 1757.

BLIGH, William (1754–1817)
100 Lambeth Road, SE1

English Admiral who was the Captain of HMS *Bounty* at the time of the famous mutiny. He entered the Royal Navy in 1762 and was the Master of HMS *Resolution* on Cook's last expedition. Appointed to command HMS *Bounty* in 1787 to transplant bread fruit trees from Tahiti to the West Indies. After sailing from Tahiti, the ship was seized by Fletcher Christian, Bligh and 18 other members of the crew being set adrift in the longboat. Bligh reached Timor after a remarkable voyage of nearly 4,000 miles in an open boat. He was promoted rear-admiral in 1811 and vice-admiral in 1814. He died in London and is buried in St Mary's, Lambeth.

BLOOMFIELD, Robert (1766–1823)
Kent House, Telegraph Street, EC2

Poet, born at Honington, Suffolk. Came to London at the age of fifteen

SIMON BOLIVAR
EL LIBERTADOR
THE GREAT LATIN AMERICAN
STATESMAN AND PATRIOT
WHO LIBERATED
BOLIVIA COLOMBIA
ECUADOR PANAMA
PERU & VENEZUELA
stayed in this house in
· 1810 ·

and became a shoemaker's apprentice. Published the popular *Farmer's Boy* in 1800 but died in poverty.

BOLIVAR, Simon, 'The Liberator' (1783–1830)
4 Duke Street, W1

Latin American statesman and patriot, born in Caracas, Venezuela, of a noble and wealthy family. Lived in Spain for three years where he married a distant cousin. He took his bride back to Caracas but she died soon after their arrival. Bolivar was active in the movements for independence of the Spanish colonies in Latin America. Venezuela declared its independence in 1811 and two years later Bolivar proclaimed himself dictator. In 1821 he became president of Colombia, which comprised Venezuela, Colombia, and New Granada, to which Ecuador was added in 1822. In 1824 he drove the Spaniards out of Peru. Upper Peru then became a separate state and was renamed Bolivia in his honour. He died at Santa Marta in Colombia and is buried in the National Pantheon, Caracas.

BOOTH, Charles (1840–1916)

6 Grenville Place, SW7

Social reformer, born in Liverpool. Founded the Booth Steamship Company with his brother Alfred, as well as the leather factories. Settled in London in 1875 and became deeply concerned about the living conditions of the working classes in the city. His *Life and Labour of the People in London* was published in 1903. President of the Royal Statistical Society 1892–4 and a Fellow of the Royal Society. Privy

Councillor 1904. He was married to Mary Macaulay, a niece of the historian.

BOSWELL, James (1740–95)

122 Great Portland Street, W1

Writer and biographer. Born in Edinburgh, the son of Lord Auchinleck, a leading advocate. Educating at Edinburgh High School and at the Universities of Edinburgh, Glasgow, and Utrecht. Admitted to the Scottish bar in 1766. Came to London and was introduced to Dr Johnson (see p. 79) in Tom Davies' bookshop in Russell Street on 16 May 1763. His first book was *An Account of Corsica* (1768) and the following year he married his cousin Margaret Montgomerie. In 1773 he was elected to the Club, whose members also included Johnson, Goldsmith, and Sir Joshua Reynolds (see p. 123), and that same year embarked on a tour of Scotland with Johnson described in

his *Journal of a Tour to the Hebrides* (1785). In 1789 he took up residence in London. Since Johnson's death in 1784 he had been putting together his *Life of Samuel Johnson*, published in 1791.

BRIGHT, Richard (1789–1858)

11 Savile Row, W1

Physician, born in Bristol. He took his MD in Edinburgh. Bright worked at Guy's Hospital in London and became the most eminent physician of his time. His studies on renal diseases led to the discovery of what today is called Bright's disease. He died in London.

BROOKE, Sir Charles (1874–1963)

13 Albion Street, W2

Colonial administrator. He succeeded his uncle, Sir James Brooke (1803–68), as second Rajah of Sarawak.

BRUCKNER, Anton (1824–96)

City Gate House, 39–45 Finsbury Square, EC2

Austrian composer, born at Ansfelden. Educated at the monastery of St Florian, where he eventually became organist in 1848. Studied in Vienna before becoming organist at Linz Cathedral. Professor of Composition at the Vienna Conservatory 1867 to 1891. Visited London twice. His works include sacred pieces, such as his *Te Deum*, as well as his more famous symphonies. He died in Vienna.

BRUMMELL, George Bryan, called Beau (1778–1840)

4 Chesterfield Street, W1

Born in London, son of Lord North's private secretary. Educated at Eton and (briefly) Oriel College, Oxford. Spent four years in the army. Inheriting a fortune from his father,

he entered on his true metier as the arbiter of good taste in dress, in which he was helped by his friendship with the Prince of Wales, the future George IV. He later quarrelled with the prince and, beset by gambling debts, was forced to flee to Calais, where he lived for fourteen years until his death in March 1840 in the pauper lunatic asylum of the Bon Sauveur in Caen.

BUCKINGHAM, George Villiers, 2nd Duke (1627–87)

2 College Hill, EC4

Born at Wallingford House (where the Admiralty now stands). His father, the 1st Duke, was assassinated and George was brought up with the children of Charles I. Embraced the royalist cause during the Civil War and following the battle of Worcester

went into exile. He returned secretly to England in 1657 to marry the daughter of the parliamentary general Lord Fairfax, who had been assigned Buckingham's forfeited estates. These were restored to him at the Restoration of Charles II, at whose court Buckingham was a prominent wit and debauchee who epitomized the lax morals of the Restoration period. In 1667 he killed the Earl of Shrewsbury in a duel. He was the author of several comedies, including *The Rehearsal* (1671). He died in miserable circumstances in 1687 at Kirby Moorside.

BURGOYNE, John (1722–92)
10 Hertford Street, W1

English general and dramatist. He bought his first commission in 1740. Three years later he eloped with a daughter of Lord Derby. He saw action during the Seven Years War, taking part in two raids on the French Coast, and subsequently went to Portugal commanding a Light Cavalry regiment. During the American Revolution he was second-in-command to Lord Careton and was forced to capitulate at Saratoga in October 1777. As a dramatist he wrote such well-known plays as *The Heiress* (1786) and *The Maid of the Oaks* (1775). He died in London.

BURKE, Edmund (1729–97)
37 Gerrard Street, W1

Statesman, author, and philosopher.

Born in Dublin, educated at Trinity College. Entered the Middle Temple in 1750 but abandoned the law for literary work. His first published work was *A Vindication of Natural Society* (1756). His *Philosophical Inquiry into the Sublime and Beautiful* appeared the same year. With the publisher Dodsley he founded the *Annual Register* in 1759 and wrote the yearly survey of events until 1788. He entered Parliament in 1765 as the Member for Wendover and showed his great rhetorical powers in the debates on the American colonies. He championed the cause of Catholic emancipation and free trade with Ireland, which lost him the Bristol seat he had won in 1774. He returned to Parliament as the Member for Malton in Yorkshire in 1781. In 1790 he published his best-known work, *Reflections on the French Revolution*. He is remembered as one of the greatest of all English orators. Lived here from 1787 to 1790.

C

CAMPBELL, Colen (1676–1729)

76 Brook Street, W1

English architect. He was a friend of
the Earl of Burlington, for whom he
designed the facade of the Royal
Academy (today replaced by a new
one by Bank and Barry). He was also
a surveyor for the Naval Hospital at
Greenwich. He achieved fame
through his designs for country
houses. His *Vitruvius Britannicus*
was published, in three volumes,
between 1715 and 1725.

**CANALETTO, (Antonio Canal,
1697–1768)**

41 Beak Street, W1

Painter, born in Venice. He was
trained by his father, a painter of
theatrical scenery. His paintings were
known in England through the
British Consul, Joseph Smith, who
bought some of them for the British
Crown. Canaletto lived in London for
nine years and painted country
houses and London scenes. He died
in his native Venice.

CANNING, George (1770–1827)

50 Berkeley Square, W1

English statesman, born in London,
brought up by his wealthy uncle,
Stratford Canning. Educated at Eton
and Christ Church, Oxford. Entered

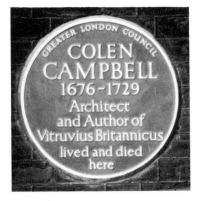

Lincoln's Inn in 1790; entered Parliament in 1794 at the suggestion of Burke (see p. 25) and became a supporter of William Pitt (see p. 118). Spoke out strongly against the slave trade and opposed peace with the French Directory. Contributed to the *Anti-Jacobin* in 1797–8. Married the sister of the Duke of Portland in 1800, who brought with her an immense fortune. Treasurer of the navy 1804–6; minister for foreign affairs in the Portland ministry of 1807. A misunderstanding with Lord Castlereagh led to a famous duel in which Canning was wounded in the thigh. After Castlereagh's suicide in 1822 Canning once again became minister for foreign affairs and became particularly active in matters concerning Latin America. Formed an administration in 1827 but died that year at the house of the Duke of Devonshire in Chiswick, in the room where Charles James Fox had died

twenty-one years earlier. Canning is buried in Westminster Abbey.

CARLYLE, Thomas (1795–1881)

24 Cheyne Row, SW3

Writer and critic, born in Ecclefechan, Dumfriesshire, the son of a stonemason. Educated at Annan Academy and Edinburgh University. Began studying for the ministry but then became a teacher of mathematics, first at Annan, then at a school in Kirkcaldy. He gave up teaching and supported himself by giving private tuition and writing for the *Edinburgh Encyclopedia*. Began to immerse himself in German literature, especially the writings of Goethe, whose *Wilhelm Meister* he later translated. Married Jane Baillie Welsh in 1826 and settled in Craigenputtock in 1828. Wrote for

the *Edinburgh Review* and for
Fraser's Magazine, to which he
contributed *Sartor Resartus*,
published in book form in 1838. In
1834 the Carlyles settled in London
at 5 (now 24) Cheyne Row. *The
French Revolution* appeared in 1837,
Heroes and Hero-Worship in 1841.
Amongst his later works were *Past
and Present* (1843), an edition of
Cromwell's Letters and Speeches
(1845), and the immense biography
of *Frederick the Great* (1858–65).
Mrs Carlyle died in 1866, after which
Carlyle wrote little of any
consequence. He died in Cheyne Row
and is buried in the churchyard at
Ecclefechan.

CASLON, William (1692–1766)

21–3 Chiswell Street, EC1

Typefounder, born in Cradley,
Worcestershire. After being
apprenticed to a London engraver he
set up his own shop. He eventually

became a letter designer and
typefounder. From 1720 to 1780,
almost every work printed in
England used type from the Caslon
foundry. His descendants operated
the foundry for almost 150 years,
until it was destroyed during the
Second World War.

CATHARINE OF ARAGON (1485–1536)

Cardinal's Wharf, Bankside, SE1

Born in Alcalà de Henares, fourth
daughter of Ferdinand and Isabella of
Castile. In November 1501 she
married Prince Arthur, the son of
Henry VII of England. By the
following April she was a widow, and
a month later she became betrothed
to her brother-in-law, the future
Henry VIII, then eleven years old.
The marriage took place, by special

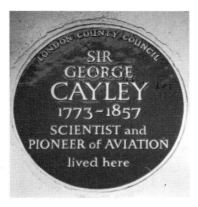

dispensation of the Pope, in June 1509, soon after Henry ascended the throne. Catharine bore Henry five children, only one of whom — the future Queen Mary — survived. In 1527, as a result of his infatuation with Anne Boleyn, Henry began to question the legality of their union, being such near relatives. The marriage was nullified by Archbishop Cranmer in 1533. Catharine spent her last days at Kimbolton Castle, Huntingdonshire (now Cambridgeshire), where she died.

See also Sir Christopher Wren (p. 162).

CAVENDISH, Henry (1731–1810)
11 Bedford Square, WC1

Natural philosopher, born in Nice, the eldest son of Lord Charles Cavendish. Educated at Peterhouse, Cambridge, which he left without taking a degree. His work on electricity anticipated the molecular theory of heat. He also measured the density and mass of the Earth. He was made a fellow of the Royal Society and Foreign Associate of the Institut de France. His name was given to the Cavendish Laboratory of Experimental Physics, Cambridge.

CAYLEY, Sir George (1773–1857)
20 Hertford Street, W1

Scientist, born at Scarborough, Yorkshire. He devoted much of his life to aeronautical research and is the founder of the science of aerodynamics. He built two full-size gliders, one of them the first man-carrying glider in history, designed an aircraft with fixed wings, and established the principles of modern aviation development. He also founded the Polytechnic Institution in Regent Street.

CHALLONER, Richard (1691–1781)
44 Old Gloucester Street, WC1

English prelate, born at Lewes,
Sussex. Educated at the English
College in Douai, ordained 1716,
professor of theology at Douai until
1730. Consecrated Bishop of Debra in
1741 and Vicar Apostolic of the
London district in 1758. Evicted from
his home during the 'No Popery' riots
of 1780 and was forced into hiding.
His works include *The Catholic
Christian Instructed* (1737) and a
revision of the Douai version of the
Bible (5 vols., 1750).

CHAMBERLAIN, (Arthur) Neville (1869–1940)

37 Eaton Square, SW1

British prime minister, son of Joseph
Chamberlain (1836–1914) by his
second marriage. Lord Mayor of
Birmingham 1915–16; chancellor of
the Exchequer 1923–4. Became
prime minister in 1937 and pursued

a disastrous policy of appeasement
with regard to the belligerent
ambitions of Hitler. The invasion of
Poland forced him to declare war on
Germany and he resigned the
premiership in 1940 in favour of
Winston Churchill (see p. 33).

CHAPLIN, Charles Spencer (1889–1978)

287 Kennington Road, SE11

Comedian, actor, film director, and
composer, born in London of
theatrical parents. Became a member
of Fred Karno's company and went
with it to Hollywood in 1914.
Immediately began making films and
quickly established the bowler-
hatted/tramp image that is forever
associated with him. After the
Second World War his left-wing
sympathies forced him to leave
America and he settled in
Switzerland, where he died.

CHATTERTON, Thomas (1752–70)

39 Brooke Street, SW3

Poet, born in Bristol. Chatterton invented the persona of Thomas Rowley, a fictitious 15th-century poet whose work was accepted as genuine by several eminent figures until the hoax was finally exposed by Thomas Tyrwhitt in 1777. The poems remain, however, works of considerable achievement. Chatterton came to London in 1770 and took lodgings in Shoreditch with the intention of making a living as a writer. Four months later, in August of that year, oppressed by loneliness and poverty, he committed suicide by taking poison in the garret of this house in Brooke Street. He was just seventeen. His death fired the imagination of several Romantic poets, including Keats, Shelley and Southey, and he was described by Wordsworth as 'the sleepless soul that perished in his pride'.

CHESTERTON, Gilbert Keith (1874–1936)

11 Warwick Gardens, W14

Essayist, novelist, poet, and critic, born in London. Educated at St

Paul's School and afterwards attended the Slade School of Art. Became a prolific journalist. His first two books were verse, *The Wild Knight* and *Greybeards at Play* (1900). He married Frances Blogg the following year. *The Napoleon of Notting Hill Gate* appeared in 1904 and this was followed by fluent and inspiring works of criticism such as his study of *Dickens* (1906) and the still vibrant *Orthodoxy* (1906) in which Chesterton described his view of Christianity. After moving out of London to Beaconsfield, Chesterton began writing the Father Brown detective stories, beginning with *The Innocence of Father Brown* in 1911. *The Victorian Age in Literature* appeared in 1913. In 1922 he was received into the Roman Catholic Church by his friend Father O'Connor, who was the original of Father Brown. A succession of religious books followed: *St Francis of Assisi* in 1923, *The Everlasting*

Man in 1925. His *Collected Poems* appeared in 1927. He died at Beaconsfield.

32 Sheffield Terrace, W8

Chesterton was born here on 29 May 1874.

CHOPIN, Frederic (1810–49)

4 St James's Place, SW1

Polish composer and pianist, born near Warsaw. He first played in public at the age of eight and published his first musical composition in 1825 when he was fifteen. Studied at the Warsaw Conservatoire 1826–9 and went to Paris in 1831. There he became famous. In 1836 he met Aurore Dudevant (George Sand), with whom he had a liaison until 1847, living with her in Majorca and at her home in Nohant. Chopin visited England in 1837 and again in 1848. He died in Paris of consumption a year later. Chopin wrote little orchestral music, the bulk of his compositions being for the piano, including two sonatas.

CHURCHILL, Lord Randolph Henry Spencer (1849–95)

2 Connaught Place, W2

Statesman, born at Blenheim Palace, Woodstock, third son of the 7th Duke of Marlborough. Educated at Eton and Merton College, Oxford. Married Jeanette (Jennie) Jerome, the daughter of a wealthy American businessman, in 1874, and in that same year was returned to Parliament as the Member for Woodstock. In 1880 he became the focus of an energetic group of younger Conservative politicians, the so-called Fourth Party. Secretary for India under Lord Salisbury and later chancellor of the Exchequer and Leader of the House. Resigned in

minister and entered on the greatest phase of his career as an inspiring and indomitable war leader. He was defeated in the 1945 election but returned as premier from 1951 to 1955. He was awarded the Nobel Prize for literature in 1950. His published works include *Marlborough* (4 vols., 1933–8) and *History of the English-Speaking Peoples* (4 vols., 1956–8). He is buried in Bladon churchyard near Blenheim.

34 Eccleston Square, SW1

Churchill lived here.

28 Hyde Park Gate, SW7

Churchill died here, 24 January 1965.

December 1886. He died in London.

CHURCHILL, Sir Winston Leonard Spencer (1874–1965)

3 Sussex Square, W2

Statesman, born at Blenheim Palace, Woodstock, eldest son of Lord Randolph Churchill (see previous entry). Educated at Harrow and Sandhurst. In 1895 he was gazetted to the 4th Hussars. Served with the Nile Expeditionary Force in 1898 and was a war correspondent during the South African campaign. Entered Parliament in 1900 as a Conservative but became a Liberal in 1906. Home secretary 1910 and the following year became first lord of the admiralty. During the First World War he was widely blamed for the Dardanelles disaster. Minister of munitions in 1917 under Lloyd George. Chancellor of the Exchequer from 1924 to 1929. In May 1940 he succeeded Neville Chamberlain (see p. 30) as prime

CLARENCE, Duke of (later William IV, 1765–1837)

22 Charles Street, W1

Third son of George III, born at

CLIVE of INDIA
1725-1774
SOLDIER AND
ADMINISTRATOR
lived here

Buckingham Palace. Created Duke of Clarence in 1789. From 1790 to 1811 he lived with the actress Mrs Jordan, by whom he had ten children. In 1818 he married Adelaide of Saxe-Meiningen and succeeded to the throne as William IV on the death of his brother George IV in June 1830. Known as the 'Sailor King' because of his career in the navy, which he joined in 1779. He was succeeded by his niece, Victoria, in June 1837.

CLIVE, Robert (1725–74)

45 Berkeley Square, W1

Soldier and administrator, born at Styche in Shropshire. Went to Madras at the age of eighteen to work as a clerk for the East India Company. He tried twice to commit suicide, after which he joined the army. In 1751 he seized Arcot and held it for eleven days against a large opposing force of Indians and French. The victories of Arni, Kaveripak, Kovilam, and Chingalpat followed. He married Margaret Maskeleyne in 1753 and returned with her to England. Two years later he was back in India and

after the massacre of the Black Hole he took Calcutta, Chandernagore, and won the battle of Plassey in June 1757. Returning to England he entered Parliament as the Member for Shrewsbury in 1761 and was raised to the Irish peerage in 1762, but in 1765 he was back in India attempting to bring order back into the East India Company's chaotic affairs. He left India for good two years later. In 1772 he was accused of taking bribes from Indian princes and defended himself brilliantly before the House of Commons. By now dependent on opium, Clive took his own life in London on 22 November 1774.

COBDEN-SANDERSON, Thomas James (1840–1922)

15 Upper Mall, W6

Printer, bookbinder, and typographer, colleague of William Morris, founder of the Doves Press. Lived here.

COLE, Sir Henry (1808–82)

3 Elm Row, NW3

Writer and art critic, and originator of the Christmas card. Born in Bath. Progenitor of the Great Exhibition of 1851. He was Chairman of the Society of Arts and founded the South Kensington Museum (now the Victoria and Albert) and became its first director in 1860.

COLERIDGE, Samuel Taylor (1772–1834)

7 Addison Bridge Place, W14

Poet and philosopher, born at Ottery St Mary, Devon. Educated at Christ's Hospital and Jesus College, Cambridge. An enthusiast of the French Revolution, he met the poet Robert Southey and hatched a scheme, called Pantisocracy, to live in a utopian democratic community on the banks of the Susquehanna River in America. In 1795, in the full flood of his enthusiasm, he married Sara Fricker whilst Southey married her sister Edith. That same year he met William Wordsworth and collaborated with him on the seminal *Lyrical Ballads* (1798), which contained Coleridge's 'Rime of the Ancient Mariner'. He settled for a time at Keswick and in 1804

travelled to Malta and Italy. He returned in poor health and addicted to opium. The latter part of his life was passed in the houses of various friends, such as John Morgan at Hammersmith and the surgeon James Gillman in Highgate. His works include a translation of Schiller's *Wallenstein* (1800), *Biographia*

Literaria and *Sybilline Leaves*
(1817), and *Aids to Reflection*
(1825). He died in the house of his
friend Gillman on 25 July 1834.

COLERIDGE-TAYLOR, Samuel (1875–1921)

30 Dagnall Park, South Norwood SE25

Composer, son of a West African
doctor and and English mother. Born
in London. Began to play the violin
at the age of five and in 1891 was
sent to the Royal College of Music.
His most famous composition,
Hiawatha (1898–1900) was inspired
by Longfellow's poem. Its
performance at the Royal Albert Hall
met with immediate success. He died
in Croydon.

COLLINSON, Peter (1694–1768)

The Ridgeway, Mill Hill, NW7

Botanist and naturalist, born at

Hugal Hall near Windermere.
Introduced American plant species
into Britain and British species into
America.

CONRAD, Joseph (1857–1924)

17 Gillingham Street, SW1

Novelist, born of Polish parents at
Berdichev. Joined an English
merchant ship in 1878 and became a
naturalized British citizen in 1884.
Gained a master's certificate and
sailed extensively in the China seas,
which provided a wealth of
background for his novels and stories.
He also went to Africa, which
provided the setting for *Heart of
Darkness*. He married in 1896 and
settled at Ashford in Kent. His first
novel, *Almayer's Folly*, was
published in 1894, followed by *An
Outcast of the Islands* (1896), *The
Nigger of the Narcissus* (1897), *Lord
Jim* (1900), *Chance* (1914), and
Nostromo (1904), which was set in

South America. Lived here.

CONSTABLE, John (1776–1837)

40 Well Walk, NW3

Painter, born at East Bergholt,
Suffolk, son of a landowner and
miller. On the suggestion of Sir
George Beaumont he was sent to
London and entered the Royal
Academy school in 1799. Married
Mary Bicknell in 1816. His *Haywain*
was the success of the Paris Salon in
1821. Elected A.R.A. in 1819, and
R.A. ten years later. His later years,
after the deaths of his wife and his
friend Archdeacon Fisher, were
clouded by depression, though he
remained financially independent.

COOK, James (1728–79)

88 Mile End Road, E1

Navigator and explorer, born at
Marton-in-Cleveland, Yorkshire.
Apprenticed to a shipowner at

Whitby at the age of eighteen and
spent several years in the coastal and
Baltic trade. Joined the navy in
1755, becoming master in 1759.
Commanded the *Endeavour*
1768–71, circumnavigated and
charted New Zealand and took
possession of the east coast of
Australia. Undertook a second voyage
of discovery 1772–5 in the
Resolution and *Adventure* to the
Antarctic. On his last voyage,

On this site
stood a house occupied
for some years by
CAPTAIN JAMES COOK. R.N. F.R.S.
1728 – 1779
Circumnavigator and Explorer

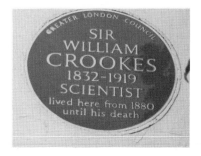

1776-9, Cook set out to find a passage round the north coast of America from the Pacific. He reached Hawaii in January 1779 where he was killed by natives.

CROOKES, Sir William (1832–1919)

7 Kensington Park Gardens, W11

Scientist, born in London. Discoverer of the element Thalium in 1861 and the sodium amalgamation process in 1865. Inventor of the radiometer and founder-editor of *Chemical News* in 1859. His published work includes *Select Methods of Chemical Analysis* (1871).

CRUDEN, Alexander (1699–1770)

45 Camden Passage, N1

Bookseller and scholar, born in Aberdeen. Came to London in 1719 and opened a bookshop in 1732, becoming bookseller to Queen Caroline three years later. In 1736 he began to compile the biblical concordance that bears his name. He made no money from the enterprise and was twice confined in a madhouse. He died here in 1770.

CRUIKSHANK, George (1792–1878)

69 Amwell Street, EC1

Engraver and illustrator. Born in

London, the son of the caricaturist Isaac Cruikshank. His talent for visual satire was shown in *The Scourge* (1811–16). He also supplied coloured etchings to *The Humorist* (1819–21) and *Points of Humour* (1823–4). He is best remembered for his illustrations to Dickens's *Oliver*

Twist and to the novels of Harrison Ainsworth, such as *The Tower of London* (1840) and *Windsor Castle* (1843). He is buried in St Paul's.

CURTIS, William (1746–99)

51 Gracechurch Street, EC3

Botanist and entomologist. Translator of Linnaeus's *Fundamenta Entomologiae* (1772).

D

DANCE, George, The Younger (1741–1825)

91 Gower Street, WC1

Architect, born in London, the son of George Dance the Elder, also an architect. Succeeded his father as City architect and surveyor. Best known as the designer of the Mansion House (1739). Also designed Blackfriars Bridge and supervised the rebuilding of Newgate Prison. Dance was a founder member of the Royal Society.

DARWIN, Charles (1809–82)

Biological Science Building, University College, 110 Gower Street, WC1

Naturalist. Born in Shrewsbury. Educated at Shrewsbury School, Edinburgh University, and Christ's College, Cambridge. At Cambridge he made the acquaintance of the distinguished botanist Henslow, who obtained a place for Darwin as naturalist to the survey ship HMS *Beagle*. Darwin sailed in December 1831, returning in October 1836. The places visited by the *Beagle* included Brazil, the Galapagos Islands, New Zealand, and Tasmania. Darwin was secretary of the Geological Society from 1838 to 1841 and in 1839 married his cousin Emma Wedgwood. Settled at Down, in Kent, from 1842 and began to develop his theory of the origin of the species. His great work, *The*

Origin of Species by Means of Natural Selection was published in November 1859 and was followed by other complementary works, including *The Descent of Man* (1871). Darwin was buried in Westminster Abbey.

DEFOE, Daniel (1661–1731)

95 Stoke Newington Church Street, N16

Author and journalist, born in London, the son of a Cripplegate butcher. Educated at a dissenting school in Newington. Defoe threw in his lot with the Duke of Monmouth and subsequently escaped punishment to become a supporter of William III. After a colourful career as a merchant, adventurer, and spy Defoe became a political writer, his best known works in this field begin *The True-Born Englishman* (1701) and *The Shortest Way with the Dissenters*, the irony of which was

misunderstood resulting in Defoe's being pilloried, fined, and imprisoned. *The Life and Strange Surprising Adventures of Robinson Crusoe of York, Mariner* appeared in 1719 and was followed by *Further Adventures of Robinson Crusoe* in the same year. *Moll Flanders* and *Journal of the Plague Year* appeared in 1722.

DE GAULLE, Charles André Joseph Marie (1890–1970)

4 Carlton Gardens, SW1

French soldier and statesman. Born in Lille. Educated at the military school at St Cyr and joined the 33rd Infantry Regiment and saw action at Verdun. He attempted to revitalize and modernize the French army, as outlined in his book *The Army of the Future* (1940). When France fell to the Nazis in June 1940 De Gaulle escaped to England to organize the Free French resistance. De Gaulle

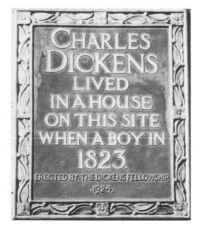

Pickwick Papers he enjoyed early literary success. In 1836 he married Catherine Hogarth, who bore him ten children between 1837 and 1852. *Oliver Twist* appeared in 1837–9, followed by *Nicholas Nickleby* (1838–9), *The Old Curiosity Shop* (1840–1), *Barnaby Rudge* (1841), *Martin Chuzzlewit* (1843), *Dombey and Son* (1846–8), *David Copperfield* (1849–50), *Bleak House* (1852–3), *Hard Times* (1854), *Little Dorrit* (1855–7), *Great Expectations* (1860–1), *Our Mutual Friend* (1864–5), and the unfinished *Mystery of Edwin Drood* (1870). After 1841 Dickens spent a good deal of time abroad, in America, Genoa, and Lausanne. He died at his home at Gadshill, near Rochester in Kent, on 9 June 1870 and is buried in Westminster Abbey.

BMA House, Tavistock Square, WC1

Dickens lived in Tavistock House,

entered Paris in August 1944 at the head of the liberating army and became head of the provisional government. He was elected first president of the Fifth Republic in 1958 and under him Algeria obtained its independence in 1962. He resigned from power in 1969 and died the following year.

DICKENS, Charles (1812–70)

141 Bayham Street, NW1

Novelist, born at Landport, near Portsmouth, the son of a clerk in the Navy Pay Office. After a hard childhood that had a permanent effect on his literary imagination he became a journalist and began his career as a writer by sending contributions to the *Monthly Magazine*. He contributed regularly to the *Evening Chronicle*, and with *Sketches by Boz* (1836) and *The*

near this site, from November 1851 to July 1860.

DISRAELI, Benjamin, 1st Earl of Beaconsfield (1804−81)

22 Theobald's Road, WC1

Statesman and novelist, born in London of Italian-Jewish descent. Educated at Blackheath and Higham Hall in Epping Forest. His first novel, *Vivian Grey* (1826), was a great success. After being defeated in four elections he was eventually returned to Parliament as MP for Maidstone in 1837. Two years later he married Mrs Wyndham Lewis (*nee* Mary Anne Lewis), a widow twelve years his senior. The couple settled at her house at 93 Park Lane. During the brief administration of Lord Derby in 1852 he was chancellor of the Exchequer and leader of the lower house. He returned to power with Lord Derby in 1858 and was again chancellor in the third Derby administration in 1866. In February 1868 he succeeded Lord Derby as prime minister, resigned in December, and again resumed the premiership in 1874. It was from this date that his close relationship with Queen Victoria began. He was defeated in the election of 1880 and retired to Hughenden, his home near High Wycombe, where he is buried. His best-known novels are *Coningsby* (1844) and *Sybil* (1846).

DOUGLAS, (George) Norman (1868−1952)

53 Albany Mansions, Albert Bridge Road, SW11

Scottish writer whose publications included novels, natural history, and travel books. Lived here.

DOWSON, Ernest Christopher (1867−1900)

1 Dowson Court, Belmont Grove, SE13

Poet, born at Lee in Kent. Educated at Queen's College, Oxford. Began working for his father, a dry-dock owner in the East End. Dowson later went to France where he scratched a living as a translator. A consumptive and alcoholic, Dowson typifies the decadent trend of the late 19th century. His best-known poem is 'Cynara' containing the line 'I have been faithful to thee, Cynara, in my fashion.' His work includes *Verses* (1896) and the poetic drama *The Pierrot of the Minute* (1897).

DOYLE, Sir Arthur Conan (1859–1930)

12 Tennison Road, SE25

Novelist and short-story writer, creator of Sherlock Holmes. Born in Edinburgh. His uncle was the artist Richard Doyle. Educated at Stonyhurst and Edinburgh University. He qualified as a doctor and had a practice at Southsea from 1882 to 1890. Sherlock Holmes was first introduced in *A Study in Scarlet* in 1882 but did not fully capture the public imagination until individual stories were serialized in the *Strand* magazine, beginning with 'A Scandal in Bohemia' in 1891, and collected as *The Adventures of Sherlock Holmes* (1892). Further adventures of Holmes and his trusty companion Dr Watson (modelled on Dr Joseph Bell, whom Doyle had known as a medical student) were published in *The Memoirs of Sherlock Holmes* (1894), *The Hound of the Baskervilles* (1902), *The Return of Sherlock Holmes* (1905), *His Last Bow* (1917), and *The Case-Book of Sherlock Holmes* (1927). Doyle also wrote historical adventures such as *The White Company* (1890), *Sir Nigel* (1906), and *The Exploits of Brigadier Gerard* (1895) and scientific romances like *The Lost World* (1912) and *The Poison Belt* (1913), which feature the character

and Achitophel (1681), *Mac Flecknoe* (1684), *Annus Mirabilis* (1667), and *Marriage à la Mode* (1694). He married Lady Elizabeth Howard in 1663 and two years later succeeded Sir William Davenant as Poet Laureate. His last work, *Fables, Ancient and Modern*, was published late in 1699, just before his death in April 1700. He is buried in Westminster Abbey.

of Professor Challenger. Doyle was knighted in 1902 and in his later years became deeply interested in spiritualism and psychic phenomena.

DRYDEN, John (1631–1700)

43 Gerrard Street, W1

Poet and dramatist, born at Aldwinkle, Northamptonshire. Educated at Westminster School and Trinity College, Cambridge. After taking his degree he came to London where he first worked as a secretary to his cousin, Sir Gilbert Pickering, who was in Cromwell's service. Although his first work, *Heroic Stanzas*, was dedicated to Cromwell he subsequently modified his political views and eventually established himself as the chief poet of the Restoration court. His works include *All for Love* (1678), *Essay of Dramatick Poesie* (1668), *Absalom*

DU MAURIER, George Louis Palmella Busson (1834–96)

New Grove House, 28 Hampstead Grove, NW3

Artist and novelist, born in Paris. Studied chemistry at University College, London, 1851, and art in Paris 1856–7. Moved to London in 1860 and quickly established himself as a capable and adaptable illustrator, providing illustrations for editions of such disparate works as Thackeray's *History of Henry Esmond* and *Foxe's Book of Martyrs*. His work also appeared in *Once a Week* and the *Cornhill Magazine*. But Du Maurier is particularly associated with *Punch*, for which he started drawing in 1860, becoming known as the principal visual satirist of the fashionable society of the time. His most successful novel, which he also illustrated, was *Trilby*, published in 1894 and featuring the character of Svengali.

E

EARNSHAW, Thomas (1749–1829)

119 High Holborn, WC1

Watchmaker. Earnshaw was the first to produce chronometers for general use and was also the inventor of the marine chronometer and the cylindrical balance spring.

EASTLAKE, Sir Charles Lock (1793–1865)

7 Fitzroy Square, W1

Painter, born in Plymouth. First director of the National Gallery and author of *Materials for the History of Oil Painting* (1847). Lived here.

EDDINGTON, Sir Arthur Stanley (1882–1944)

4 Bennett Park, SE3

Astonomer and mathematician. Born at Kendal. Educated at Owen College, Manchester, and Trinity College, Cambridge. Chief assistant at the Royal Observatory at Greenwich 1906 to 1913 and succeeded Sir Robert Ball as Plumian professor of astronomy and experimental philosophy at Cambridge. Author of *Space, Time and Gravitation* (1920), *Stars and Atoms* (1927), and *The Expanding Universe* (1933). Knighted in 1930 and received the Order of Merit in 1938.

EDWARDS, Edward (1812–86)

11 Idol Lane, EC3

Librarian, originator of free library legislation and first librarian of the Manchester Free Library. His works

include *Memoirs of Libraries* (1859) and a biography of Sir Walter Raleigh (1865).

EISENHOWER, Dwight David (1890–1969)

20 Grosvenor Square, W1

American soldier and statesman, born in Denison, Texas, the son of a railroad worker. Entered West Point military academy, graduating in 1915. Chief military assistant to General McArthur in the Philippines at the outbreak of the Second World War and in 1942 became commander of the allied

assault on North Africa. In 1944 he was selected as supreme commander of the allied invasion of Europe known as 'Operation Overlord'. Elected president of the USA in 1952 by a large majority and re-elected in 1956. His publications include *Crusade in Europe* (1948) and an autobiography, *At Ease* (1968).

ELGAR, Sir Edward (1857–1934)

51 Avonmore Road, W14

English composer, born at Broadheath, near Worcester, son of a Roman Catholic music dealer and organist. Succeeded his father as organist of the Roman Catholic church in Worcester. Married Caroline Roberts in 1889 and moved to London. Settled in Malvern two years later to concentrate on composing. Established his reputation with the *Enigma Variations* (1899) and the oratorio *The Dream of Gerontius* (1900). He was knighted in 1904 and awarded the Order of Merit in 1911 – the first musician to receive the OM. Master of the King's Musick from 1924. Elgar

was largely responsible for revitalizing English music and giving it an international standing.

42 Netherhall Gardens, NW3

Elgar lived in a house on this site from 1911 to 1921 and composed *The Music Makers, Falstaff,* and *The Spirit of England* here.

ELIOT, George (Mary Ann Cross, *née* Evans, 1819–80)

31 Wimbledon Park Road, SW18

Novelist born at Arbury Farm near Nuneaton, Warwickshire, educated at a school in Coventry. Began to write for the *Westminster Review* in 1850 and met the philosopher Herbert Spencer and the critic George Henry Lewes. She lived with Lewes from 1854 until his death in 1878. In May 1880 she married John Cross, with whom she lived until her death in December of that year. She was buried in Highgate Cemetery. Her works include *Adam Bede* (1858), *The Mill on the Floss* (1860), *Silas Marner* (1861), *Middlemarch* (1871–2), and *Daniel Deronda* (1875–6).

4 Cheyne Walk, SW3

George Eliot died here 22 December 1880.

ELIOT, Thomas Stearns (1888–1965)

Thornhaugh Street, WC1

Poet and critic, born in St Louis, Missouri. Spent four years at Harvard and then went to Paris before returning to Harvard. Won a travelling scholarship to Oxford and was persuaded by Ezra Pound to remain in England. Become a naturalized citizen in 1927. Taught for a time, then worked in a bank before joining the publishing firm of Faber and Faber. The first volume of Eliot's poems, *Prufrock and Other Observations*, was published in 1917. *The Waste Land* appeared in the first number of *The Criterion* in 1922. The poem won the prestigious Dial Award and brought Eliot 2000 dollars. *Ash Wednesday* was published in 1930 and *Four Quartets* in 1943. Eliot also wrote poetic dramas, beginning with *Sweeney Agonistes* in 1932, followed by *Murder in the Cathedral* (1935), *The Family Reunion* (1939), and *The Cocktail Party* (1949). His critical works include *The Sacred Wood* (1920), *The Use of Poetry and the Use of Criticism* (1933), and *Notes Towards a Definition of Culture* (1948). He also produced a classic book of poetry for children, *Old Possum's Book of Practical Cats* (1939). He was awarded the Nobel Prize for Literature in 1948 and the Order of Merit the same year. Eliot worked here for Faber and Faber from 1925 to 1965.

Kensington Court Palace, Kensington Court Gardens, W8

Eliot died here on 4 January 1965.

ELLIS, Henry Havelock (1859–1939)

14 Dover Mansions, Canterbury, Crescent, SW9

Pioneer in the scientific study of sex. Born in London, studied medicine at St Thomas's Hospital. Author of the 7-volume *Studies in the Psychology of Sex* (1897–1928) and founder of the Mermaid series of Elizabethan and Jacobean dramatists.

ENGELS, Friedrich (1820–95)

121 Regent's Park Road, NW1

Political philosopher, born in Barmen, Germany, the son of a wealthy manufacturer. From 1842 he lived mainly in England. In 1844 he met Karl Marx (see p. 96) in

Brussels and that same year his influential book *Condition of the Working Classes in England* was published. Collaborated with Marx on the *Communist Manifesto*, published in 1848, and spent much of his later life editing and translating the works of Marx. He died in London and is buried in Highgate Cemetery.

EPSTEIN, Sir Jacob (1880–1959)

18 Hyde Park Gate, SW7

Sculptor, born in New York of Russian-Polish parents. Educated in New York and at the Ecole des Beaux Arts in Paris. Eventually settled in England, where he spent most of the rest of his life. Commissioned to produce eighteen figures for the facade of the British Medical Council building in the Strand, 1907–8, and *Night* and *Day* for the London Transport building (1929). Among his many portrait heads are those of

George Bernard Shaw, T.S. Eliot, Somerset Maugham, and Albert Einstein. Other notable pieces by Epstein include his *Christ in Majesty* at Llandaff Cathedral and *St Michael and the Devil* for Coventry Cathedral. He was knighted in 1954 and died in London.

EWART, William (1798–1869)

16 Eaton Place, SW1

Politician and reformer, born in Liverpool. Called to the bar in 1827 and entered Parliament. A committed opponent of capital punishment. In 1834 he carried through a bill to abolish hanging in chains and three years later secured support for an act abolishing capital punishment for cattle stealing. Ewart was also responsible for initiating a scheme to commemorate eminent persons, first implemented by the Royal Society of Arts which erected a plaque to Lord Byron at 24 Holles Street.

F

FARADAY, Michael (1791–1867)
48 Blandford Street, W1

Scientist, born at Newington Butts, the son of a blacksmith. Apprenticed to a bookbinder and then became assistant to Humphry Davy at the Royal Institute. Married Sarah Barnard in 1821. His most important discoveries arose out of his researches into electricity and include induced electricity in 1831, the relation of electric and magnetic forces in 1838, and atmospheric magnetism in 1851. His famous Christmas lectures at the Royal Institution attracted wide audiences. He became advisor to Trinity House and in 1862 introduced the use of magneto-electric light in lighthouses.

He retired in 1858 and lived near Hampton Court, where he died.

FAWCETT, Dame Millicent (*née* Garrett, 1847–1929)
2 Gower Street, WC1

Reformer, born at Aldeburgh, Suffolk, sister of Elizabeth Garrett Anderson (see p. 12). In 1867 she married Henry Fawcett, professor of political economy at Cambridge and a Liberal MP. After his death in 1884 she lived in London with her sister Agnes and her daughter Philippe. She was a committed supporter of political rights for women and was president of the Women's Unionist Association. She was awarded the GBE in 1925.

FITZROY, Robert (1805–65)

38 Onslow Square, SW7

Admiral, hydrographer, and
meteorologist, born at Ampton Hall,
Suffolk. Entered the navy in 1819
and saw service in the Mediterranean
and in the South Atlantic. Took
command of HMS *Beagle* in 1828 and
surveyed the coasts of Patagonia and
Tierra del Fuego. Commanded the
Beagle again in 1831 on the
expedition of which Charles Darwin
(see p. 40) was a member. The
Fitzroy barometer was named after
him. He became governor of New
Zealand in 1843 and was promoted to
vice-admiral in 1863. He committed
suicide two years later.

FLAXMAN, John (1755–1826)

7 Greenwell Street, W1

Sculptor, born in York, where his
father was a moulder of plaster
figures. Studied at the Royal
Academy and later provided
Wedgwood with designs for their
pottery. Studied in Rome 1787–94.
Professor of sculpture at the Royal
Academy 1810. Examples of his
statues can be seen in Westminster
Abbey (e.g. John Kemble) and in St
Paul's (e.g. Sir Joshua Reynolds).
Flaxman died in a house on this site
on 7 December 1826.

FLECKER, James Elroy (1884–1915)

9 Gilmore Road, SE13

Poet, born in Lewisham. Studied
oriental languages at Cambridge.
Author of *Hassan* (performed in
1923) and *The Golden Journey to
Samarkand* (1913). Born here.

FLEMING, Sir Alexander (1881–1955)

20a Danvers Street, SW3

Bacteriologist, born in Loudon,
Ayrshire. Educated at Kilmarnock

Academy and St Mary's Hospital medical school. Served as a captain in the Royal Army Medical Corps during the First World War. Took up his research into anti-bacterial substances after the war and in 1928 discovered penicillin by chance, although it was not until 1942 that a method was discovered of producing the drug. Fleming shared the Nobel Prize for Medicine in 1945 with Sir Howard Florey and Ernst Chain.

FLEMING, Sir John Ambrose (1849–1945)

9 Clifton Gardens, W9

Physicist, born in Lancaster. Professor of electrical engineering at University College, London, consultant to the Bell and Marconi companies. Inventor of the thermionic valve. Knighted in 1929.

FLINDERS, Captain Matthew (1774–1814)

56 Fitzroy Street, W1

Explorer, born at Donington, Lincolnshire. Entered the royal navy at fifteen and from 1795 to 1799 explored the Australian coastline and circumnavigated Tasmania. Discovered the Bass Strait with George Bass. Commissioned to circumnavigate Australia in 1801. He was shipwrecked on the return journey and captured by the French. The Flinders River in Queensland and the Flinders range of mountains are named after him. He published an account of his travels in *A Voyage to Terra Australis* (1814).

FORSTER, Edward Morgan (1879–1970)

9 Arlington Park Mansions, Turnham Green Terrace, W4

Novelist, born in London. Educated at Tonbridge School, where he was bitterly unhappy, and King's College, Cambridge, where he met G.E.

Moore, G. Lowes Dickinson, and G.M. Trevelyan. Founded the *Independent Review* with Dickinson, whose biography he wrote. After taking his degree Forster went to Italy, which inspired *Where Angels Fear to Tread* (1905) and *A Room With a View* (1908). His next novel, *Howards End*, appeared in 1910. His experiences in India provided the background for *A Passage to India* (1924), which was a great success. Forster also published collections of stories, such as *The Celestial Omnibus* (1914) and *The Eternal Moment* (1928), and essays, including *Abinger Harvest* (1936) and *Three Cheers for Democracy* (1951). He also published an influential critical work, *Aspects of the Novel*, in 1927. He was made an honorary fellow of King's and received the Order of Merit in 1968. His homosexual novel *Maurice*, written 1913–14, was published posthumously in 1971.

Fox, Charles James (1749–1806)

46 Clarges Street, W1

Stateman, born in Westminster, third son of the 1st Lord Holland. Educated at Eton and Hertford College, Oxford. Become MP for Midhurst at the age of nineteen. A supporter of Lord North, who made him lord of the admiralty. During the American War of Independence Fox was a strenuous opponent of the government's policy of coercion and an even stronger opposer of the policies pursued by his arch-enemy William Pitt (see p. 118), especially with regard to pursuing the war with revolutionary France. When Pitt died in 1806 Fox was called to office and began to negotiate peace terms with France; he was also on the point of introducing anti-slavery legislation when he died suddenly at Chiswick. Burke (see p. 25) called Fox 'the greatest debater the world ever saw': he was also one of the greatest

began publishing *Poor Richard's Almanack*. Began his famous researches into electricity in 1746. A prime mover of the Declaration of Independence in 1776, Franklin was a key negotiator with both England and France and in 1778 secured a treaty of alliance with the latter. Twice president of the state of Pennsylvania. On his death the French Assembly went into mourning for three days.

FREUD, Sigmund (1856–1939)
20 Maresfield Gardens, NW3

Psychoanalyst, born in Freiberg, Moravia, of Jewish parents. Studied medicine in Vienna and under Charcot in Paris. With the Viennese physician Josef Breuer he published *Studien über Hysterie* in 1895. Abandoning the hypnotic techniques he had learnt from Charcot, Freud developed the method of free association to elicit material from his

gamblers and drinkers of his time. He was buried in Westminster Abbey, uncomfortably close to Pitt.

FRANKLIN, Benjamin (1706–90)
36 Craven Street, Strand, WC2

American statesman and scientist, born in Boston, Mass. Apprenticed at the age of twelve to his brother James, who was a printer and publisher of the *New England Courant*, to which Benjamin contributed. Became acquainted with Sir William Keith who sent him to London on an abortive business trip in 1724. He remained there for eighteen months, working as a printer, and then returned to Philadelphia. In 1729 he bought the *Pennsylvania Gazette* and in 1732

patients and from this became convinced that infantile sexuality held the key to neurosis and dream interpretation. His seminal work *The Interpretation of Dreams (Die Traumdeutung)* appeared in 1900. The Vienna Psychoanalytical Society was founded in 1908 and the International Psychoanalytical Association, with C.G. Jung as its first president, in 1910. Both Jung and Alfred Adler, another member of the IPA, moved away from the central Freudian hypothesis to develop psychologies of their own. In 1933 psychoanalysis was banned by the Nazis and Freud and his family settled in Hampstead, where he died of cancer of the jaw in September 1939.

FRIESE–GREENE, William (1855–1921)

136 Maida Vale, W9

Photographer and motion-picture pioneer, born in Bristol. Moved to London in 1885 to set up a photographic studio. Began to experiment with moving pictures and in 1889 patented the first motion-picture camera, which used celluloid film. Friese-Greene's ideas were many years ahead of his time: he even suggested to Edison that his moving-picture camera and Edison's phonograph could be linked to produce talking pictures – an innovation that was not achieved commercially for forty years. He is buried in Highgate Cemetery.

FRY, Elizabeth (1780–1845)

Entrance to St Mildred's Court, Poultry, EC2

Quaker and prison reformer. Born in Norwich, daughter of a wealthy merchant and banker. Married Joseph Fry, a London merchant, in 1800. Became a Quaker preacher and in 1813 visited Newgate, which inspired her to devote her life to prison reform, both in England and abroad. She also founded hostels for the homeless.

G

GAINSBOROUGH, Thomas (1727–88)

82 Pall Mall, SW1

Landscape and portrait painter. Born Sudbury, Suffolk. Sent to London to study under Gravelot and Hayman. In 1745 he married Margaret Burr, natural daughter of the Duke of Beaufort. Settled in Ipswich and began painting portraits – e.g. *Mr and Mrs Andrews* (1748). Moved to Bath in 1760 and began to attract a large number of fashionable sitters. Founder-member of the Royal Academy, 1768. Painted portraits of George III and Queen Charlotte in 1781 and in 1785 produced his famous portrait of the actress Mrs Siddons. He also produced landscapes, such as *The Morning Walk* (1780) and *Cattle Crossing a Bridge* (1781).

GAITSKELL, Hugh Todd Naylor (1906–63)

18 Frognal Gardens, NW3

British Labour politician, born in London. Educated at Winchester and New College, Oxford. Reader in political economy at London University, 1938. Became MP for Leeds South in 1945; chancellor of the exchequer 1950–1. His introduction of health service charges led to a long rift with Aneurin Bevan and left-wing members of the party. Elected leader of the opposition in 1955, defeating Bevan. Author of *Money and Everyday Life* (1939). Lived here.

GALTON, Sir Francis (1822–1911)

42 Rutland Gate, SW7

Scientist and explorer, born near Sparkbrook, Birmingham. Educated at King Edward's School, Birmingham Hospital, and at Cambridge and London Universities. Travelled extensively from 1846 to

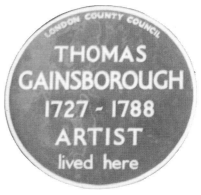

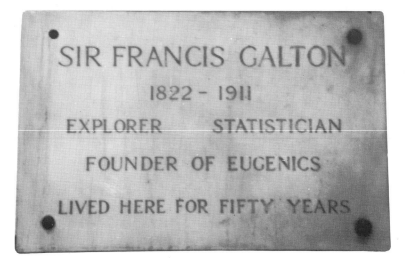

1850, including North Africa and
South Africa. Published *Narrative of
an Explorer in Tropical South
Africa* in 1855. Also investigated
meteorology, heredity, and eugenics.
His *English Men of Science: Their
Nature and Nurture* appeared in
1874. Fellow of the Royal Society,
1856. Knighted in 1909. He died in
Haselmere.

GANDHI, Mohandas Karamchand (1869–1948)

Kingsley Hall, Powis Road, E3

Indian leader, born at Porbandar,
Kathiawar, of a Hindu family. Came
to London to study law at the age of
eighteen. Called to the bar in 1891.
Returned to India and practised as a
lawyer in Bombay. Went to South
Africa in 1893 and became involved
in opposition to discriminatory
legislation against Indians. He had
now abandoned his lucrative legal
practice and dedicated himself to the
political liberation of his
countrymen. He was soon the
leading figure in the Congress
organization and engineered the civil

disobedience campaign of 1920. He was jailed for two years in 1922. In 1930 he led a famous 200-mile march to the sea to collect salt – a symbolic gesture of defiance against the government monopoly of this commodity. Arrested again but released in 1931. Re-arrested many times subsequently. Assassinated in Delhi by a Hindu fanatic in January 1948, a year after India achieved independence.

GAUDIER-BRZESKA, Henri (1891–1915)

454 Fulham Road, SW6

Sculptor and artist, born at St Jean-de-Braye, Loire. Largely self-educated, but studied art on a scholarship in Bristol. Patronized by Ezra Pound and through Wyndham Lewis, became associated with the Vorticist movement. Killed in combat during the First World War at Neuville-St-Vaast.

GIBBON, Edward (1737–94)

7 Bentinck Street, W1

Historian, born in Putney, educated at Westminster and Magdalen College, Oxford, holding a low opinion of both institutions. Became a Roman Catholic when he was sixteen. Sent to Lausanne where he was brought back into the Protestant fold by a Calvinist pastor – as described in his *Autobiography* (1796). He returned to England in 1758 and in 1761 published *Essai sur l'Etude de la Litterature* (English edition, 1764). From 1759 to 1763 he was a captain in the Hampshire militia and then, in the following year, 'musing among the ruins of the Capitol' in Rome, he was struck by the idea of writing what was to become his *magnum opus*, *The Decline and Fall of the Roman Empire*, the first volume of which appeared in 1776. Entered Parliament in 1774. The second and

third volumes of *Decline and Fall*
were published in 1781; the last
three volumes were written in
Lausanne and completed on the
night of 27 June 1787. He died in
London.

GLADSTONE, William Ewart (1809–98)

Eglinton Road School, Plumstead, SE18

Statesman, born in Liverpool, of
Scottish descent. Educated at Eton
and Christ Church, Oxford; president
of the Oxford Union. Conservative
MP for Newark, 1832. Junior lord to
the treasury and then under-
secretary for the colonies under Peel.
During the debate on Disraeli's
budget in 1852 Gladstone showed
himself to be a supreme
parliamentary orator. The Liberals
came to power in 1868 and
Gladstone, who had by now
abandoned his high Tory principles,
became prime minister and
instituted a number of important
reforms, including a programme of
national education. In all, Gladstone
enjoyed four terms as premier. He
finally resigned in March 1894 and
retired to Hawarden, where he died
on 19 May 1898. He is buried in
Westminster Abbey.

GLAISHER, James (1809–1903)

20 Dartmouth Hill, EC4

Meteorologist, born in London.
Involved with the Ordnance Survey
of Ireland, chief meteorologist at
Greenwich in 1829. Founded the
Royal Meteorological Society in 1850.
Glaisher made several high altitude
balloon ascents. His famous dew

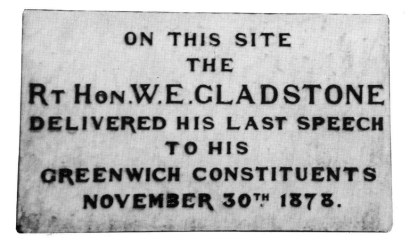

ON THIS SITE
THE
RT HON.W.E.GLADSTONE
DELIVERED HIS LAST SPEECH
TO HIS
GREENWICH CONSTITUENTS
NOVEMBER 30TH 1878.

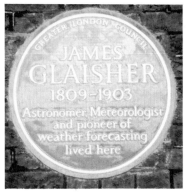 

point tables were published in 1845.
He died in Croydon.

GODWIN, George (1813–88)

24 Alexander Square, SW7

Architect, journalist, and social
reformer. Lived here.

GOSSE, Sir Edmund William (1849–1928)

56 Mortimer Road, Hackney, N1

Poet and critic, son of the naturalist
Philip Henry Gosse (1810–88). Their
relationship is described in detail in
Father and Son (1907). Assistant
Librarian at the British Museum
1867–75 and librarian to the House
of Lords 1904–14. Wrote on a wide
variety of literary topics, including
studies of John Donne (1899), Sir
Thomas Browne (1905), and
Swinburne, introduced the plays of
Ibsen to English readers, and
published two volumes of poems.
Born here 21 September 1849.

GOUNOD, Charles Francois (1818–93)

15 Morden Road, SE3

French composer, born in Paris.
Studied at the Conservatoire and in
Rome. Organist of the Missions
Etrangères, where his *Messe
solonnelle* was first performed. He
achieved success with his comic
opera based on Molière's play,
Médecin malgré lui (1858). But it
was *Faust* (1859) which brought him
fame, and this was followed by
Philemon et Baucis in 1860 and
Romeo et Juliette in 1867. He left
France for England during the
Franco-Prussian War of 1870 and
composed his biblical elegy *Gallia* for
the opening of the Albert Hall. He
died at St Cloud.

GRACE, William Gilbert (1848–1915)

Mottingham Lane, SE12

Cricketer, born at Downend, Bristol.

Obtained a medical degree in 1879. Twice captain of England. By 1895 he had scored a hundred centuries. Lived here.

GRAHAME, Kenneth (1859–1932)

16 Phillimore Place, W8

Author, born in Edinburgh, educated at St Edward's School, Oxford. Entered the Bank of England in 1879. Maried Elspeth Thomson in 1899 and the couple settled here. Published *Pagan Papers* in 1893, followed by *The Golden Age* in 1895, and *Dream Days* in 1898. His masterpiece, *The Wind in the Willows*, appeared in 1908 and has become one of the handful of genuine children's classics.

GRAY, Thomas (1716–71)

39 Cornhill, EC3

Poet and scholar, born in London in a house on this site, son of a

prosperous scrivener. Educated at Eton and Peterhouse, Cambridge, where he first met Horace Walpole (see p. 153). In 1739 he accompanied Walpole on the Grand Tour for two and a half years but quarrelled with him at Reggio. Gray returned to England and in 1742 wrote his *Ode on a Distant Prospect of Eton College*. His great *Elegy Written in a Country Churchyard* was published in 1751. By this time he was back at Peterhouse, migrating across the road to Pembroke in 1765. In 1768 he became a professor of history and modern languages in the university and enjoyed the dual reputation of a distinguished scholar and the leading poet of his time. He died in his rooms at Pembroke and is buried beside his mother in the churchyard at Stoke Poges.

GREEN, John Richard (1837–83)

4 Beaumont Street, W1

Historian. Born in Oxford. Educated at Magdalen College School and Jesus College, Oxford. Took holy orders and in 1866 became incumbent of St Philip's, Stepney. Three years later he became librarian at Lambeth, a post he held until he renounced orders in 1877 due to his liberal theological views. His *Short History of the English People* was published in 1874.

St Philip's Vicarage, Newark Street, E1

Green lived here from 1866 to 1869.

GREY, Edward, Viscount Grey of Falloden (1862–1933)

1 Queen Anne's Gate, SW1

Foreign Secretary at time of start of

First World War; spoke the famous words 'The lamps are going out all over Europe; we shall not see them lit again in our lifetime'. Lived in 3 Queen Anne's Gate (now part of No. 1) from 1906 to 1913.

GROTE, George (1794–1871)

12 Savile Row, W1

Historian and politician, born at Clay Hill, near Beckenham, Kent. Educated at Charterhouse and became a clerk in the family bank in 1810. In his spare time he studied widely – especially classics, literature, and political economy. Became MP for the City of London in 1832. Retired from banking – having become head of the firm in 1830 – in 1843 and devoted himself to writing. His *History of Greece* was published in 1846–1856. Grote became vice-chancellor of London University in 1862. He is buried in Westminster Abbey.

GWYNNE, Nell (*c.* 1650–87)
79 Pall Mall, SW1

Probably born in Gwynne Street, Hereford. A seller of oranges in Covent Garden before becoming an actress. She became the mistress first of Lord Buckhurst and then of Charles II, whose affection for her (and hers for him) was genuine. There was at least one son – Charles Beauclerk, Duke of St Albans – of their union. After Charles' death she rejected all other suitors. She is buried in St Martin-in-the-Fields.

H

HALDANE, Richard Burdon, 1st Viscount (1856–1928)

28 Queen Anne's Gate, SW1

Statesman, philosopher, and lawyer. Educated at the universities of Edinburgh and Gottingen. Called to the bar in 1879 and that same year entered Parliament as a Liberal. Founder of the territorial army. Lord chancellor 1912–15; awarded the Order of Merit in 1915.

HANDEL, George Frederick (1685–1759)

25 Brook Street, W1

Composer and musician, born at Halle, Lower Saxony. Became organist of Halle Cathedral when he was seventeen. Spent four years in Italy and in 1710 took up an appointment at the court of the Elector of Hanover. Came often to England, which displeased the Elector, to try to establish himself: his opera *Rinaldo* was performed in 1711. The Elector ascended the English throne as George I in 1714 and Handel is supposed to have composed the *Water Music* in an attempt to placate him. Handel wrote 32 oratorios, including *Saul* (1739) and *Messiah* (1742). He is buried in Westminster Abbey.

HANSOM, Joseph Aloysius (1803–82)

27 Sumner Place, SW7

Architect and inventor, born in York. Designed the Birmingham Town Hall. In 1836 he invented the safety cab carrying his name. Hansom also designed a number of churches, including the Roman Catholic cathedral in Plymouth.

HARDY, Thomas (1840–1928)

172 Trinity Road, SW17

Novelist and poet, born at Upper Bockhampton, Dorset, the son of a stonemason. In 1856 he was articled to the architect John Hicks in Dorchester who specialized in ecclesiastical commissions. Hardy went to London when he was twenty-two to pursue his career in architecture. At the same time he began to write. His first novel, *Desperate Remedies*, appeared in 1871, followed by *Under the Greenwood Tree* (1872) and *A Pair of Blue Eyes* (1873). The first novel to reveal Hardy's greatness was *Far*

From the Madding Crowd in 1874. Four years later came *The Return of the Native*. After settling at Max Gate in Dorchester, which he had designed himself, he published *The Mayor of Casterbridge* (1886), *Tess of the D'Urbervilles* (1891), and *Jude the Obscure* (1895). Hardy also published collections of short stories, such as *Wessex Tales* (1888) and *Life's Little Ironies* (1894), and in the latter part of his life concentrated on poetry, such as *Time's Laughing Stocks* (1910) and *Satires of Circumstance* (1914). He married twice, to Emma Giffird in 1874 and after her death, to Florence Dugdale in 1914. He was awarded the Order of Merit in 1910.

HARMSWORTH, Alfred Charles William, 1st Viscount Northcliffe (1865–1922)

31 Pandora Road, NW6

Journalist and newspaper magnate,

permanently in London. In 1759 he constructed a large marine chronometer, which when tested during a voyage to Jamaica from 1761 to 1762 erred by only 18 geographical miles. This achievement entitled him to collect a £20,000 reward set up by Act of Parliament in 1714. It was only in 1773, through George III's personal intervention, that Harrison was paid in full. He died in London in 1776.

HARTE, Francis Bret (1836–1902)

74 Lancaster Gate, W2

American author, born in Albany, N.Y. He was forced to leave school and seek work at the age of thirteen. He went to California in 1854 and there worked for a number of papers. In 1868 he was appointed first editor of the *Overland Monthly* and was commissioned to write some local sketches. *The Luck of Roaring Camp*

born in Chapelizod, Dublin. Began his career as a freelance journalist and eventually became editor of *Youth*. Started *Answers to Correspondents* in 1888 and *Comic Cuts* in 1890, as well as other cheap popular periodicals. In 1896 came the *Daily Mail*, followed by the *Daily Mirror* in 1903. In 1908 Northcliffe took over *The Times* and lowered its price by a penny to increase its circulation. He was created a baronet in 1904 and was raised to the peerage in 1906.

HARRISON, John (1693–1776)

Summit House, Red Lion Square, WC1

Inventor, born at Foulby, near Pontefract, Yorkshire. He lived at Barrow-upon-Humber, Lincolnshire, from 1700 to 1736, when he settled

and *The Outcasts of Poker Flat* made him famous overnight. He went to Glasgow in 1880 serving as US Consul there until 1885, when he retired to London, where he died.

Hawkins, Sir Anthony Hope (1863–1933)

41 Bedford Square, WC1

Novelist who wrote under the name 'Anthony Hope'. Educated at

Marlborough and Balliol College, Oxford. Called to the bar at the Middle Temple in 1877. Remembered now for his 'Ruritanian' adventures, beginning with *The Prisoner of Zenda* (1894). Knighted in 1918.

Hawthorne, Nathaniel (1804–64)

4 Pond Road, SE3

American author, born in Salem, Mass. Educated at Bowdoin College, Brunswick, Maine. His first collection of short stories, *Twice-Told Tales*, appeared in 1837. He married Sophia Peabody in 1842 and the couple settled at the Old Manse in Concord, Mass. There he wrote *Mosses from an Old Manse* (1846). *The Scarlet Letter*, published in 1850, made him famous, and this was followed by *The House of the Seven Gables* (1851). When his friend Franklin Pierce was elected President he appointed Hawthorne US consul in Liverpool, a post Hawthorne resigned at the end of Pierce's administration. A year and a half spent in Italy furnished material for *The Marble Faun* (1860). He returned to Concord and began contributing to the *Atlantic Monthly* a series of pieces on England, collected as *Our Old Home* in 1863. His other works include *Wonder Book* (1851) and its sequel *Tanglewood Tales* (1853).

HAZLITT, William (1778–1830)

6 Bouverie Street, EC4

Journalist and essayist, born at Maidstone, Kent. He first tried his hand at portrait painting (Charles Lamb, best man at his wedding, was one of his subjects), but then turned to journalism on the *Morning Chronicle* and Leigh Hunt's *Examiner*. From 1814 to 1830 he contributed to the *Edinburgh Review*. His *Round Table* essays and *Characters of Shakespeare's Plays* appeared in 1817 and his magisterial

The Spirit of the Age in 1825. He was buried in St Anne's, Soho, destroyed during a German air raid in the Second World War.

6 Frith Street, W1

Hazlitt died here on 18 September 1830.

HEINE, Heinrich (1799–1856)

32 Craven Street, WC2

German poet and essayist. Born in Dusseldorf of Jewish parentage. Educated at Bonn, Berlin, and Gottingen. In 1835 he became a Christian to secure the rights of German citizenship. After the revolution of 1830 he migrated to Paris, where he spent the remainder of his life. He is best remembered for

his lyrical poetry, in particular the
Buch der Lieder (1827).

HENDERSON, Arthur (1863–1935)

13 Rodenhurst Road, SW4

Statesman, born in Glasgow.
Chairman of the Labour Party three
times. Home secretary in 1924,
foreign secretary 1929–31. President
of the World Disarmament
Conference, 1932. He was awarded

the Nobel Peace Prize in 1934. Died
in London.

HERZEN, Alexander (1812–70)

1 Orsett Terrace, W2

Russian political thinker and writer,
born in Moscow. Imprisoned for his
revolutionary views in 1834. Settled
in London in 1851, where he wrote
novels and socialist propaganda.
Founder of the paper *Kolokol*
(The Bell). Died in Paris.

HILL, Sir Rowland (1795–1879)

1 Orme Square, W2

Postal reformer, born at
Kidderminster, Worcestershire, the
son of a schoolmaster. A founder of
the Society for the Diffusion of Useful
Knowledge (1826) and a supporter of
the socialist ideals of Robert Owen.
Published *Post-Office Reform* in 1837
in which he advocated a system
based on pre-paid stamps. This led to

the introduction of the penny post in January 1840. Buried in Westminster Abbey.

Royal Free Hospital, Pond Street, NW3

Sir Rowland Hill lived here from 1849 to 1879.

HOBBS, Sir John (Jack) Berry (1882–1961)

17 Englewood Road, SW12

English cricketer. Played for Cambridgeshire in 1904, Surrey 1905–35, and for England 1907–30; captain of England in 1926. Knighted in 1953. Lived here.

HODGKIN, Thomas (1798–1866)

35 Bedford Square, WC1

Pathologist, philanthropist, and reformer, born in London. Described the glandular disease named after him. Lived here.

HOGARTH, William (1697–1764)

Hogarth House, Hogarth Lane, W4

Painter and engraver, born in London. Studied painting under Sir James Thornhill, with whose daughter he eloped in 1729. The first of his great moral series, *A Harlot's Progress*, were executed in 1730–1, followed by *A Rake's Progress* (1733–5) and *Marriage à la Mode* (1743–5). The vices of the lower classes were depicted in *Gin Lane, Beer Street*, and *The Four Stages of Cruelty* (all 1751). He is buried in Chiswick churchyard.

HOGG, Quintin (1845–1903)

5 Cavendish Square, W1

Philanthropist and educationalist, born in London, the son of a wealthy West Indian merchant. Educated at Eton. Founded the Youth's Christian Institute in 1882 which developed into the Regent Street Polytechnic. Lived here 1885–98.

HOOD, Thomas (1799–1845)

31 Poultry, EC2

Poet and humorist, born in a house on this site. He was a gifted engraver and artist but in 1822 turned to journalism as sub-editor of the *London Magazine* and made the acquaintance of such literary figures as De Quincey, William Hazlitt (see p. 69), and Charles Lamb (see p. 85). In 1825 he married the sister of John Hamilton Reynolds. From 1829 he produced *The Comic Annual* and for the Christmas 1843 number of *Punch* wrote his famous 'Song of the Shirt'. He died at Devonshire Lodge, Finchley Road, and is buried in Kensal Green cemetery.

HOPKINS, Gerard Manley (1844–89)

Manresa House, Roehampton, SW15

Poet, born in London. Educated at Balliol College, Oxford. Converted to Catholicism in 1866 and entered the Society of Jesus. Ordained priest in 1877. He was a uniquely inventive and innovative poet, though none of his poems were published in his lifetime. They first came to public attention when Robert Bridges published a full edition of them in 1918. In 1884 Hopkins became professor of Greek at Royal College (now University College), Dublin, where he died. His best-known poems include 'The Wreck of the *Deutschland*' and 'The Windhover'.

HORE-BELISHA, 1st Baron (1893–1957)

16 Stafford Place, SW1

Barrister and politician, born at Devonport. Served in France during the First World War, following which he went up to St John's College, Oxford. Called to the bar in 1923 and that year became liberal MP for Devonport. As minister for transport he introduced the 'Belisha Beacon' for pedestrians. He also drafted a new highway code and instituted driving

tests for motorists. Raised to the peerage in 1954 and died in France.

HUDSON, William Henry (1841–1922)

40 St Luke's Road, W11

Author and naturalist, born in Argentina. Became a British subject in 1900. His early writings covered the natural history of South America, but his later and better known works dealt with English subjects, such as *British Birds* (1895), *Birds in London* (1898), *Nature in Downland* (1900), *Hampshire Days* (1903), and *A Hind in Richmond Park* (1922). He died in London and is buried at Broadwater in Sussex.

HÜGEL, Baron Friedrich von (1852–1925)

4 Holford Road, NW3

Roman Catholic theologian, born in Florence. His family moved to

England in 1867 and settled in Torquay. Married Lady Mary Herbert in 1873. Von Hügel's works include *The Mystical Element in Religion* (1908–9). He died in London and left his library to St Andrews University.

HUNT, James Henry Leigh (1784–1859)

22 Upper Cheyne Row, SW3

Poet, essayist, and journalist, friend of Shelley and Keats. Born at Southgate, Middlesex, a clergyman's son; educated at Christ's Hospital. From 1808, with his brother, he edited *The Examiner*, a leading forum for liberal opinion which also published the early work of Shelley and Keats. In 1813 Hunt was imprisoned for two years for a libel on the Prince Regent. In 1822 he accompanied Byron to Italy in order to establish *The Liberal*, which did not prove a success. He returned to

England in 1825 and in 1828 published *Lord Byron and his Contemporaries*. Hunt wrote poetry (such as *The Story of Rimini*, 1816), plays, and even a novel (*Sir Ralph Esher*, 1834), but he is best remembered for his literary friendships and his sparkling essays on literary subjects. He was caricatured as Harold Skimpole by Dickens in *Bleak House*.

HUNTER, John (1728–93)

31 Golden Square, W1

Surgeon and physiologist, born at
Long Calderwood, Lanarkshire.
Educated at Chelsea Hospital and St
Bartholomew's. Entered St George's
Hospital in 1754; house surgeon
there 1756. Elected FRS 1767, and in
1776 became surgeon-extraordinary
to George III. Amongst his works is a
pioneering *Natural History of
Human Teeth* (1771–8). He also
investigated venereal disease. In 1771
he married the poetess Anne Home
(1742–1821), author of several songs
set to music by Haydn. Dr Hunter
died in London and is buried in
St Martin-in-the-Fields.

HUNTER, William (1718–83)

Lyric Theatre (rear),
Great Windmill Street, W1

Scottish anatomist and obstetrician,
brother of John Hunter (q.v.). Born
Long Calderwood, Lanarkshire.

Studied for the Church at Glasgow
University but took up medicine in
1737. Came to London in 1741 and
trained in anatomy at St George's
Hospital. Specialized in midwifery
and in 1764 was appointed
physician-extraordinary to Queen
Charlotte. FRS 1767, professor of
anatomy to the Royal Academy 1768.
In 1770 he built this house
containing a museum, a lecture
theatre, and a dissecting room. His
museum was bequeathed to the
University of Glasgow.

HUTCHINSON, Sir Jonathan
(1828–1913)

15 Cavendish Square, W1

Surgeon and scientist, born at Selby,
Yorkshire. Worked at St
Bartholomew's Hospital, London.
Described the three primary
symptoms of congenital syphilis
known as 'Hutchinson's Triad'.
Elected FRS 1882; knighted in 1908.

HUXLEY, Sir Julian Sorell (1887–1975)

31 Pond Street, NW3

Biologist, born in London, grandson of Thomas Henry Huxley (see next entry). Educated at Eton and Balliol College, Oxford. After serving in the First World War he became professor of zoology at the Royal Institution (1926–9) and secretary to the Zoological Society of London (1935–42). FRS 1938, knighted in 1958. His publications include *Essays of a Biologist* (1923), *Religion Without Revelation* (1927), and *Evolutionary Ethics* (1943). He was the first director-general of UNESCO.

HUXLEY, Thomas Henry (1825–95)

38 Marlborough Place, NW8

Biologist, born in Ealing. Attended medical school at Charing Cross Hospital. Joined the navy as a surgeon on HMS *Rattlesnake* on an expedition to the Torres Strait. Lectured on natural history at the Royal School of Mines. Became the leading supporter of Darwin's theory of evolution. His publications include *Man's Place in Nature* (1863) and *Science and Education* (1899).

I

IRVING, Washington (1783–1859)

8 Argyll Street, W1

American author, born in New York of English parents. Under the pseudonym 'Geoffrey Crayon' he published *The Sketch Book* (1819–20), a miscellany containing 'Rip Van Winkle' and 'The Legend of Sleepy Hollow'. His travels in Europe produced a number of books, including *Tales of a Traveller* (1825), *The Conquest of Granada* (1829), and *The Alhambra* (1832). In 1842 he was appointed ambassador to Spain, returning finally to the USA in 1846. He was also a gifted

biographer, writing on subjects as varied as *Oliver Goldsmith* (1846) and *Washington* (1855–9).

J

JAMES, Henry (1843–1916)
34 De Vere Gardens, W8

Novelist, born in New York, brother of the philosopher William James. Educated at Harvard. An early trip to Europe kindled a lifelong passion for European culture. He began his literary career by contributing sketches, reviews, and short stories to various periodicals, his first novel, *Watch and Ward*, appearing in 1871. This was followed by *Roderick Hudson* (1875), *Portrait of a Lady* (1881), *The Bostonians* (1886), *The*

Spoils of Poynton (1897), *What Maisie Knew* (1897), and *The Golden Bowl* (1904), all written in characteristically compressed and fastidious style. James became a British citizen in 1915 and received the Order of Merit a year later.

JEFFERIES, John Richard (1848–87)
59 Footscray Road, SE9

Naturalist and novelist, born near Swindon. Began his literary career as a journalist on the *North Wilts Herald*. His first success was *The Gamekeeper at Home* (1878), followed by *Wild Life in a Southern County* (1879) and the futuristic *After London, or Wild England* (1885). In 1883 he published his spiritual autobiography, *The Story of My Heart*.

JELLICOE, John Rushworth, 1st Earl (1859–1935)
25 Draycott Place, SW3

Admiral, born in Southampton, son of a sea captain. Joined the navy in 1872. Survived the collision of the *Victoria* and the *Camperdown* in 1893. Involved in modernizing the

fleet under Admiral Fisher.
Appointed commander-in-chief of
the Grand Fleet at the outbreak of
the First World War and caught the
German fleet off Jutland in May
1916: the Germans retreated and
their fleet did not put to sea again for
the duration of the war. Admiral of
the fleet in 1919. Governor of New
Zealand from 1920 to 1924 and
president of the British Legion
(1928–32). Created an earl in 1925.
Buried in St Paul's.

JINNAH, Mohammed Ali (1876–1948)

35 Russell Road, W14

Pakistani statesman. Educated in
Bombay and Lincoln's Inn. Called to
the bar 1897. President of the Indian
Muslim League. When Pakistan
obtained its independence from
Indian in 1947 Jinnah became its
first governor-general.

JOHNSON, Dr Samuel (1709–84)

Johnson's Court, Fleet Street, EC4

Poet, critic, and lexicographer, born
at Lichfield, Staffordshire. Educated
at Lichfield Grammar School and
Pembroke College, Oxford. In 1737,
after an abortive career as a
schoolmaster, he came to London, a
move which inspired his first poem,
London (1738). He began work on
his famous *Dictionary* in 1747
(published 1755) and in 1750
commenced publication of *The
Rambler. Rasselas*, written to defray
the expenses of his mother's funeral,
was published in 1759. In 1762 he
received a pension of £300 a year,
and the following year made the
acquaintance of his future
biographer, James Boswell, with
whom he undertook the tour
described in *Journey to the Western
Isles of Scotland* (1775). The famous
Literary Club was founded in 1764

and in 1779–81 came Johnson's last and perhaps greatest work, his *Lives of the Poets* in 10 volumes. He was buried in Westminster Abbey and there is a monument to him, erected by members of the Club, in St Paul's Cathedral. Johnson lived in a house on this site from 1765 to 1776.

Anchor Brewery, Southwark Bridge Road, SE1

Dr Johnson once occupied a room near the gatehouse.

JONES, Ernest (1879–1958)

19 York Terrace East, NW1

Psychoanalyst, born in Llwchwr, Glamorgan. Educated at Cardiff University. Became a lifelong disciple of Freud (see p. 55). Founded the British Psychoanalytical Society in 1913 and the *International Journal of Psychoanalysis* in 1920. Lived here.

K

KARSAVINA, Tamara (1885–1978)

108 Frognal, NW3

Russian ballerina, member of
Diaghilev's Ballets Russes. Lived
here.

KEATS, John (1795–1821)

Keats's House, Wentworth Place, Keats Grove, NW3

Poet, born in London, the son of a
livery stable keeper. After
apprenticeship to the surgeon in
Edmonton he qualified as a surgeon
himself. Through the friendship of
Leigh Hunt (q.v.) he was introduced
to a literary circle that included
Shelley, Charles Lamb, and William

Hazlitt (q.v.), and it was Hunt who
published Keats's famous sonnet 'On
First Looking into Chapman's Homer'
in *The Examiner*. His first volume of
Poems (1817) was not a success, but
nevertheless Keats abandoned
surgery for literature. *Endymion*
appeared in 1818 and was savagely
criticized. The 1820 volume *Lamia,
and Other Poems* is one of the high
watermarks of English poetry,
containing as it does the great odes
'To Psyche', 'To a Nightingale', 'On a
Grecian Urn', and 'To Autumn', as
well as 'La Belle Dame Sans Merci'
and 'Lamia' itself. In September
1820, suffering from consumption
and oppressed by his futile love for
Fanny Brawne, Keats sailed for Italy
with his artist friend Charles Severn,
who was with him when he died in
Rome on 23 February 1821, aged 25.

Enfield Town Station, booking hall, Enfield

John Keats's first school was in a
house on this site. Demolished 1872.

KENNEDY, John Fitzgerald (1917–63)

14 Prince's Gate SW7

American president. Born at

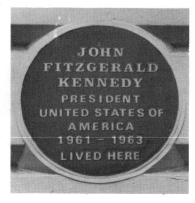

company, and with her helped to found the Vic-Wells ballet. Associated with the Bloomsbury Group of writers and artists (see p. 171). Adviser to the Treasury during both world wars. Played a leading part in establishing the International Monetary Fund. An outstanding economist, his works include *The Economic Consequences of the Peace* (1919), *A Treatise on Money* (1930), and *Essays in Persuasion* (1931). Raised to the peerage in 1942 as 1st Baron Keynes.

Brookline, Mass. His father was US ambassador in London from 1937 to 1940. During the Second World War Kennedy served as a torpedo boat commander in the Pacific, for which he was awarded the Navy Medal and the Purple Heart. He entered politics in 1947 as a Democrat and eventually became the first Roman Catholic ever to be elected president of the USA. He married Jacqueline Lee Bouvier in 1953. His firm and courageous handling of the Cuban missile crisis in 1962 looked certain to ensure his re-election, but on 22 November 1963 he was assassinated, supposedly by Lee Oswald, in Dallas.

KEYNES, John Maynard (1883–1946)

52 Gordon Square, WC1

Economist, born in Cambridge. Educated at Eton and King's College, Cambridge. Married Lydia Lopokova, a dancer with Diaghilev's ballet

KIPLING, Rudyard (1865–1936)

43 Villiers Street, WC2

Poet and author, born in Bombay. Educated in England but returned to India in 1880 to work on the Lahore *Civil and Military Gazette*. His early works include *Departmental Ditties* (1886) and *Plain Tales From the Hills* (1888). In 1889 he returned to England and settled in London.

Barrack Room Ballads (1892) was a great success. Though remembered as the great champion of British imperialism, the range of Kipling's work was far wider, from the two *Jungle Books* (1894–5) and the *Just So Stories* (1902) to *Stalky and Co* (1899), *Kim* (1901), *Puck of Pook's Hill* (1906), *Rewards and Fairies* (1910), and the autobiographical *Something of Myself* (1937). He was awarded the Nobel Prize for Literature in 1907. He died at his home, Batemans, in Sussex. Lived here from 1889 to 1891.

KITCHENER, Horatio Herbert, 1st Earl (1850–1916)

2 Carlton Gardens, SW1

Soldier and statesman, born near Ballylongford, County Kerry, of English Protestant descent. Commissioned in 1871. After taking part in the expeditionary force that attempted to rescue General Gordon, besieged in Khartoum, Kitchener was appointed Sirdar of the Egyptian army in 1890 and won the Battle of Omdurman (2 September 1898). Commander-in-chief in South Africa 1900–2. During the First World War he became secretary of state for war in Asquith's government. Lost at sea when HMS *Hampshire* was mined off Orkney on 5 June 1916.

KNOX, Edmund George Valpy (1881–1971)

110 Frognal, NW3

Essayist, poet, and parodist. Editor of *Punch* 1932–49. He published books of light verse, such as *A Little Loot* (1919) and *Parodies Regained* (1921), and collections of his humorous articles. Lived here from 1945 until his death.

KOKOSHKA, Oskar (1886–1980)

Eyre Court, Finchley Road, NW8

Painter, born at Pöchlarn in Austria. Studied in Vienna from 1904–8. Settled in England in 1938 and became a naturalized citizen in 1947. Lived here.

KOSSUTH, Louis (1802–94)

39 Chepstow Villas, W11

Hungarian patriot. Born at Monok, near Zemplin. An ardent nationalist, he insisted on the severance of all links with Austria. He was

imprisoned for his views and on his release in 1840 became the editor of *Pest Hirlap*, a forum for extreme liberal views. Lived mainly in England from 1852 to 1859, trying several times to organize mass uprisings against Austria. Retired from active political life in 1867 and settled in Turin. His *Memoirs of My Exile*, in three volumes, were published in 1880–2.

L

LAMB, Charles (1775–1834)
2 Crown Office Row, Temple, EC4

Essayist and man of letters, born here in the Temples, where his father was clerk to Samuel Salt, a wealthy bencher. Educated at Christ's Hospital 1782–9, where he formed a lifelong friendship with Coleridge. In 1792 he began employment at India House, remaining there until his retirement in 1825. In 1796 his sister Mary, in a fit of insanity, killed her mother with a table-knife and was committed to an asylum. Lamb gave up the chance of marriage to devote himself to the care of his sister, who was allowed to return home. After unsuccessfully publishing some verse Lamb was asked by William Godwin to contribute to his 'Juvenile Library', for which he prepared the now famous *Tales From Shakespeare*. He also edited selections from

Elizabethan dramatists. He is best remembered for the essays he wrote for the *London Magazine* under the name of 'Elia', the first series being published in 1823, the second in 1833. His sister, to whom he had devoted his life, survived him, dying in 1847.

Colebrook Cottage, 64 Duncan Terrace, N1

Lamb lived here from 1822 to 1827.

LANG, Andrew (1844–1912)

1 Marloes Road, W8

Scottish man of letters, specializing in books on religion and mythology, though perhaps best known for his series of *Fairy Books*. Educated at Edinburgh Academy, St Andrews University, and Balliol College, Oxford. Fellow of Merton College, Oxford, 1868. His books include *Custom and Myth* (1884), *Letters to Dead Authors* (1886), and a three-volume *History of Scotland* (1899–1904).

LANGTRY, Lillie (properly Emilie Charlotte, *née* Le Breton, 1852–1929)

21 Pont Street, SW1

Actress, born in Jersey. One of the most beautiful women of her time. married Edward Langtry in 1874 and made her first appearance on the stage in 1881. A friend of Oscar Wilde and other intellectuals and artists, she met the Prince of Wales, the future Edward VII, in 1877 and became his mistress. She was widowed in 1897 but later married Hugo de Bathe. Her reminiscences, *The Days I Knew*, were published in 1925.

LASKI, Harold Joseph (1893–1950)

5 Addison Bridge Place, W14

Political scientist and socialist, born in Manchester. Educated at Manchester Grammar School and New College, Oxford. Professor of political science at the London

School of Economics from 1920 until his death. Elected chairman of the Labour Party in 1945; later proclaimed himself a Marxist. Author of *Authority in the Modern State* (1919) and *A Grammar of Politics* (1925).

LAUDER, Sir Harry (1870–1950)

46 Longley Road, SW17

Comic singer and music-hall artiste, born in Edinburgh. His best-remembered songs, for which he wrote both the music and lyrics, include 'Roamin' in the Gloamin'', 'I Love a Lassie', and 'Keep Right on to the End of the Road'. He entertained the troops in France during the First World War and was knighted in 1919.

LAWRENCE, David Herbert (1885–1930)

1 Byron Villas, Vale of Health, NW3

Poet and novelist, born in Eastwood,

Nottinghamshire, the son of a miner and a schoolteacher. His first novel, *The White Peacock* (1911), was a success and encouraged him to give up a teaching career to become a full-time writer. *The Rainbow* was published in 1915 and Lawrence found himself prosecuted for obscenity. After 1919 he spent much of his life abroad, in Italy, Mexico, and America. His most famous novel, *Lady Chatterley's Lover*, was published in 1928 and was again the subject of an action for obscenity. Lawrence's other works include *Sons and Lovers* (1913), *Women in Love* (1921), *Kangaroo* (1923), and *The Plumed Serpent* (1926). He married Frieda von Richtofen, a cousin of the famous German air ace, in 1914. He died of tuberculosis at Vence, near Nice.

LAWRENCE, John Laird Mair, 1st Baron (1811–79)

Southgate House, High Street, Southgate, N14

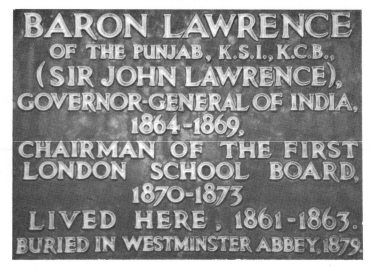

Administrator, born in Richmond, Yorkshire. Served as a judge in Calcutta and Delhi. Commissioner and lieutenant-governor of the Punjab. Succeeded Lord Elgin as governor-general of India in 1863. Returned to England in 1869 and created Baron Lawrence. Chairman of the London School Board 1870–3.

LAWRENCE, Thomas Edward (1888–1935)

14 Barton Street, SW1

Soldier, born in Wales. Educated at Jesus College, Oxford, where he read modern history. Travelled to the Middle East as a junior member of the British Museum archaeological team at Carchemish on the

Euphrates — his first contact with the desert Arabs. During the First World War he joined the intelligence service in Cairo and organized revolt against the Turks with the help of Emir Faisal. Adviser on Arab affairs

to the colonial office, becoming known as 'Lawrence of Arabia'. After the war he returned to England and joined the RAF as Aircraftsman Shaw. He was killed whilst driving a motor-cycle in May 1935. His publications included *The Seven Pillars of Wisdom* (1926), *Revolt in the Desert* (1927), and *Crusader Castles* (1936).

LECKY, William Edward Hartpole (1838–1903)

38 Onslow Gardens, SW7

Irish historian and philosopher, born near Dublin, educated at Trinity College. Became MP for Dublin University in 1895 and was awarded the Order of Merit in 1902. His works include *The Leaders of Public Opinion in Ireland* (1861) and his great *History of England in the Eighteenth Century* (1878–90). Lived here.

LEIGHTON, Frederic, 1st Baron (1830–96)

Leighton House, 12 Holland Park Road W14

Painter, born in Scarborough, Yorkshire. Studied art in a number of European cities, including Rome, Florence, Berlin, and Paris. In 1855 he exhibited his famous pastiche *Cimabue's Madonna Carried in Procession* at the Royal Academy, which was bought by Queen Victoria. Leighton was also a distinguished sculptor. In 1878 he became president of the Royal Academy and was knighted. Eight years later he was created a baronet and in 1896 became Lord Leighton of Stretton. He never married and is buried in St Paul's.

LENIN, Vladimir Ilyich (1870–1924)

Royal Scot Hotel, 100 King's Cross Road, WC1

Russian revolutionary, born in Simbirsk (Ulyanov), the son of a professor of physics and mathematics. Educated at Kazan University but took his degree in St Petrsburg. The execution of his brother by the tsarist authorities propelled him towards Marxism. Exiled to Siberia, he wrote *The Development of Capitalism in Russia* (1899). He came to London in 1902, returning the following year to attend the Third Congress of the Russian Social Democratic Labour Party. The father of Russian communism, his remains rest in Moscow's Red Square.

LISTER, Joseph, 1st Baron Lister of Lyme Regis (1827–1912)

12 Park Crescent, NW1

Surgeon, born in Upton, Essex. Educated at University College, London. Became house surgeon to James Syme, the Scottish surgeon, and married Syme's daughter Agnes in 1852. Successively Regius professor of surgery at Glasgow and professor of clinical surgery at Edinburgh. President of the Royal Society 1895–1900. Lister introduced antiseptic treatment in surgery and insisted on cleanliness and sterilization in operating theatres. Awarded the Order of Merit in 1902.

LISZT, Franz (1811–86)

18 Great Marlborough Street, W1

Composer and pianist. Visited England three times, 1824–7. Lived with the Comtesse d'Agoult by whom he had three children: one of them, Cosima, married Wagner. As a pianist, Liszt was a supreme technician. He visited London again in 1886, the year he died. He stayed in a house on this site in 1840 and 1841.

LLOYD-GEORGE, David, 1st Earl of Dwyfor (1865–1945)

3 Routh Road, SW18

Liberal statesman, born in

 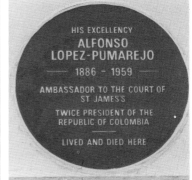

Manchester. After his uncle's death he was brought up by an uncle in Wales. Entered politics and eventually became the leading figure of the Liberal Party's radical wing. As president of the Board of Trade from 1905 to 1908 he introduced the Merchant Shipping Act and founded the Port of London Authority, and as chancellor of the Exchequer he laid the foundations of the modern welfare state. He succeeded Asquith as prime minister in 1916. According to Hitler, Lloyd-George was 'the man who won the First World War'. He was created an earl in 1945. His works include *War Memoirs* (1933–6).

LOPEZ-PUMAREJO, Alfonso (1886–1959)

33 Wilton Crescent, SW1

Colombian banker and statesman. Elected president of the Republic of Colombia in 1934 and during his first mandate, from 1934 to 1938, brought in many social and legal reforms. He was elected to the presidency again in 1942.

LYELL, Sir Charles (1797–1875)

73 Harley Street, W1

Scottish geologist, born at Kinnordy, Forfarshire, but brought up in the New Forest. Educated at Exeter College, Oxford, where he studied under Buckland and became interested in geology. Author of the seminal *Principles of Geology* (1830–3), which, with Darwin's *Evolution of the Species*, was one of the great attitude-changing books of the nineteenth century. Darwin's views were taken up in *The Geological Evidences of the Antiquity of Man* (1863). Professor of geology at King's College, London, 1832–3. Knighted in 1848 and created a baron in 1864. Lived here.

M

**MACAULAY, Thomas Babington
1st Baron (1800–59)**

**Queen Elizabeth College
(formerly Holly Lodge),
Campden Hill, W8**

Author and historian, born at
Rothley Temple, Leicestershire.
Educated at a private school and at
Trinity College, Cambridge. Called to
the bar in 1826, joining the northern
circuit. Elected Member of
Parliament (Liberal) for Edinburgh in
1834 and became Secretary for War
in Lord Melbourne's cabinet in 1839.
The first two volumes of his famous
History of England appeared in
1848; volumes 3 and 4 appeared in
1855. He was a leading contributor
to the *Edinburgh Review* for nearly
twenty years. His *Lays of Ancient
Rome* (1842) were immensely
popular, as were his *Essays*,
published in three volumes in 1843.
He was created a peer in 1857, as
Baron Macaulay of Rothley, and is
buried in Westminster Abbey.

**MACDONALD, James Ramsay
(1866–1937)**

9 Howitt Road, NW3

Politician, born at Lossiemouth, on
the Moray Firth, the son of a
labourer. A self-educated man, he
became a socialist and in 1894 joined
the Independent Labour Party. In
1896 he married Ethel Gladstone, a

niece of Lord Kelvin. MacDonald had a decisive influence on the creation of the Labour Party. Elected to Parliament for Leicester in 1906, he became leader of the Labour Party in the House of Commons in 1911. After losing his seat in 1918 and failing to get in for East Woolwich, he was returned to Parliament in 1922 and was elected leader of the Opposition. In 1924 he was called upon by the king to form a new government. His insistence on making treaties with Russia led to attacks by the press, which identified Labour with Bolshevism. The Conservatives came back in the 1924 general election with a large majority and MacDonald resigned to become once again leader of the Opposition. After the general election of May 1929 he returned to power and retained his post after the general election of 1931. He resigned in 1935 for reasons of health and died in mid-Atlantic en route to South America.

MACDOWELL, Patrick (1799–1870)

34 Wood Lane, N6

Sculptor, born in Belfast. While working in London with a coach builder he began sketching and modelling with Pierre Francois Chenu, a French sculptor. His designs and busts were exhibited at the Royal Academy, and eventually he was elected a Member. His masterpiece, *Europe*, is exhibited at the Albert Memorial, Hyde Park, while his statues of William Pitt, Earl of Chatham, and of William Pitt the Younger are in the palace of Westminster.

MCMILLAN, Margaret (1860–1931)
MCMILLAN, Rachel (1859–1917)

127 George Lane, Heather Green, SE13

Margaret McMillan, educational reformer, was born in New York and brought up near Inverness. In 1902 she joined her sister Rachel in London. Together they were responsible for opening the first school clinic in 1908 and the first open-air nursery school in 1914. The Rachel McMillan Training College, for nursery and infant teachers, was set up after her death as a memorial. Margaret was awarded the CBE in 1917 and became a CH in 1930. The sisters lived here from 1910 to 1913.

MALONE, Edmond (1741–1812)

40 Langham Street, W1

Shakespearian scholar and editor, born in Dublin, educated at Trinity College. Called to the Irish bar in 1767. Came to London in 1774 and met Samuel Johnson, Horace Walpole, and Sir Joshua Reynolds, who painted his portrait. From 1777 Malone devoted himself to literary work, in particular to the study of Shakespearean chronology. His own edition of the plays was published in 1790. He was one of the first to express scepticism concerning the authenticity of the 'Rowley' poems – see Chatterton (p. 30). Died here.

MANBY, Charles (1804–84)

60 Westbourne Terrace, W2

Civil engineer, son of Aaron Manby, designer and builder of the first iron steamship, named after him. Father and son also built the first French steamer to sail across the Atlantic, the *Caroline*.

MANSBRIDGE, Albert (1878–1952)

198 Windsor Road, Ilford

Educationist and founder of the Workers' Educational Association in 1903. Lived here.

MANSFIELD, Katherine (pen name of Kathleen Middleton Murry, *née* Beauchamp, 1888–1923)

17 East Heath Road, NW3

Writer, born in Wellington, New Zealand. Married the critic John Middleton Murry in 1918. She was a gifted writer of short stories as well as being an acute critic. Her works include *The Garden Party* (1922) and *Something Childish* (1924). Her *Collected Short Stories* appeared in 1945. She died of tuberculosis at Fontainebleau.

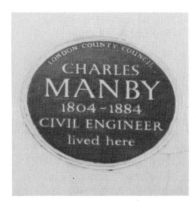

MANSON, Sir Patrick (1844–1922)

50 Welbeck Street, W1

Doctor and medical researcher, born at Oldmeldrum, Aberdeen. Studied at Marischal College, Aberdeen. Helped to found the London School of Tropical Medicine in 1899 and the Society of Tropical Disease, of which he was first president, in 1907. Known as 'Mosquito Manson' for his work on malaria.

MARCONI, Guglielmo, Marchese (1874–1937)

71 Hereford Road, W2

Inventor, pioneer of wireless communication. Born in Griffone, Italy. Educated at University of Bologna. After experiments on wireless telegraphy on his father's estates he came to London in 1896. He first sent signals across the Atlantic in 1901 and shared the Nobel Prize for physics in 1909. He died in Rome.

2 Aldersgate Street, EC1

Marconi made the first public transmission of wireless signals from here in July 1898.

MARSDEN, William (1796–1867)

65 Lincoln's Inn Fields, WC2

Surgeon, lived here.

From the roof of this building

GUGLIELMO MARCONI

made the first public transmission
of wireless signals

Under the patronage of
WILLIAM PREECE F R S
Engineer-in-Chief, the General Post Office

27 JULY 1896

MARVELL, Andrew (1621–78)

Outside Wall of Waterloo Park, West Side Highgate High Street, N6

Poet, born at Winestead, Yorkshire. Educated at Hull Grammar School and Trinity College, Cambridge, where he took his BA in 1639. He travelled to Holland, France, Italy and Spain as a tutor to a member of the Skinner family. Tutor to Lord Fairfax's daughter and subsequently to William Dutton, Cromwell's ward. On Milton's recommendation he was appointed Latin Secretary (i.e. Foreign Secretary) under the Secretary of State, John Thurloe. He wrote a number of satires, using the street ballad as a means of political propaganda, but is best remembered for his pastoral and garden poems, in particular 'To his coy Mistress'. He died in London.

MARX, Karl Heinrich (1818–83)

28 Dean Street, W1

Communist, born in Trier, Rhenish Prussia, the son of a Jewish lawyer who was afterwards baptized as a Protestant along with all the members of his family. Educated at the Universities of Bonn and Berlin, he received a doctor's degree at the University of Jena in 1841. He married Jenny von Westphalen in 1843. He was by then the editor of the *Rheunische Zeitung* in Cologne. When the newspaper was closed as a result of Marx's virulent attacks on the government the couple emigrated

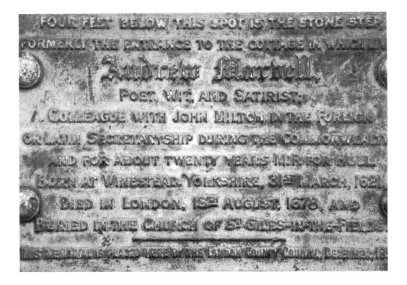

munificence. His revolutionary ideas appeared first in the *Communist Manifesto* of 1848. His most famous work, *Das Kapital* (1867), was written in the British Museum's Reading Room, Seat No. G7. Marx died in London and is buried in Highgate Cemetery.

MASARYK, Thomas Garrigue (1850–1937)

21 Platts Lane, NW3

First president of the Czechoslovak Republic, born near Hodonin, Czechoslovakia, the son of a coachman. Educated at a Czech school in Cejkovice and in Vienna, where he obtained a doctor's degree in 1876. He returned to the university in 1879 as a lecturer in

to Paris. He returned to Germany in 1848, only to be expelled once again. This time he settled in London, where he was to live for the rest of his life, often in dire poverty, alleviated by occasional journalistic activities but mainly by Engels'

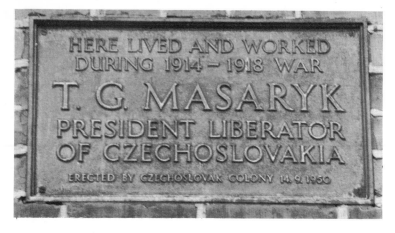

Philosophy. Masaryk's political career started in the early 1890s. He was elected to Parliament in 1891, resigned his seat in 1893, and was re-elected in 1907. He advocated his country's independence from the Austro-Hungarian Empire. During a trip to the USA in 1918 he obtained President Wilson's support for his cause, and at the end of the First World War Czechoslovakia became an independent republic with Masaryk as its first president. He was re-elected in 1920, 1927, and 1934, and resigned in 1935. His beloved pupil, Benes, was elected to succeed him.

MAUGHAM, William Somerset (1874–1965)

6 Chesterfield Street, W1

Novelist and short-story writer, born in Paris. Educated at King's School, Canterbury, Heidelberg University,

and St Thomas's Hospital where he received his MD degree. His experiences in the London slums as a medical student were drawn on in *Liza of Lambeth* (1897). During the First World War he served in the intelligence service, which formed the background for his spy story *Ashenden* (1928). Married Lady Wellcome, the daughter of Dr

Barnardo (see p. 16) in 1915, but they were divorced in 1927. Settled in Cap Ferrat in 1930 but lost most of his possessions when the Germans invaded. His novels include *Of Human Bondage* (1915), *The Moon and Sixpence* (1919), *The Painted Veil* (1925), *Cakes and Ale* (1930), *The Razor's Edge* (1945), and *Catalina* (1948). He is also known for his short stories, collected together in three volumes in 1951, and wrote several plays. He was made a Companion of Honour in 1954.

MAXIM, Sir Hiram Stevens (1840–1916)

57d Hatton Garden, EC1

Inventor and engineer, born in Sangersville, Maine, USA. He settled in London where he invented his famous machine gun. He took British nationality and founded the Maxim Gun Company. He was knighted in 1901 and died in Streatham.

MAZZINI, Giuseppe (1805–72)

10 Laystall Street, EC1

Italian patriot, born in Genoa. Educated at the University of Genoa, where he graduated in law. An ardent patriot, he fought for Italy's liberation from both foreign and domestic tyranny. In 1837 he came to London where he wrote articles for the *Edinburgh Review, Westminster Review*, and others. From London he organized several attempted risings as well as the Society of the Friends of Italy. He died in Pisa.

MEREDITH, George (1828–1909)

7 Holbury Street, SW10

Poet and novelist, born in Portsmouth. Educated privately and in Germany. After being articled to a solicitor he became a journalist and

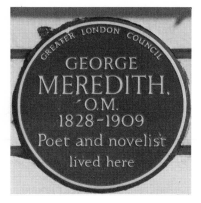

in 1849 married Mary Ellen Nicolls, the widowed daughter of the writer Thomas Love Peacock. He wrote regularly for *The Fortnightly* and was also a reader for the publishing firm of Chapman and Hall. His first novel, the oriental fantasy *The Shaving of Shagpat*, appeared in 1855 and was followed by *The Ordeal of Richard Feverel* (1859), *Evan Harrington (1860), Harry Richmond* (1871), *Beauchamp's Career* (1876), *The Egoist* (1879), *Diana of the Crossways* (1885), and *The Amazing Marriage* (1895). Meredith was also a distinctive poet, remembered especially for the sonnet sequence *Modern Love* (1862). His wife eloped with Henry Wallis in 1858 and in 1864 Meredith married Marie Vulliamy. He died at Box Hill in Surrey.

METTERNICH, Prince Clemens Lothar Wenzel (1773–1859)

44 Eaton Square, SW1

Austrian statesman and diplomat, born in Coblenz. During a long stay in England he made the acquaintance of the Prince of Wales (the future George IV). In 1795 he married Countess Eleonore von Kaunitz. In 1809 he was appointed Minister of Foreign Affairs, remaining in office for forty years. After Napoleon's defeat Metternich presided, along with Castlereagh and Talleyrand, over the Congress of Vienna. A wholehearted reactionary, Metternich used the Holy Alliance to fight liberalism in Austria, Germany, and Italy. After his resignation in 1848 Metternich came to England, living in Brighton and London. He returned to Vienna in 1851, where he died eight years later.

MILL, John Stuart (1806–73)

18 Kensington Square, W8

Philosopher and reformer, born in London, the son of James Mill, a

Rossetti in the formation of the Pre-Raphaelite movement. His *Christ in the House of His Parents* (1850) was considered blasphemous and violently attacked. *The Blind Girl* (1856) and *Chill October* (1871) offer two contrasting examples of his work. Millais was created a baronet in 1885 and elected president of the Royal Academy in 1896. He is buried in St Paul's Cathedral.

MILNER, Alfred 1st Viscount (1854–1925)

14 Manchester Square, W1

Statesman, born in Bonn. Educated at Tubingen, King's College, London, and Balliol College, Oxford, where he graduated in 1877. Called to the bar at the Inner Temple in 1881 and joined the staff of the *Pall Mall Gazette*. In 1889 he was appointed Under Secretary of Finance in Egypt. After four years there he returned to England and wrote *England in*

prominent historian, economist, and philosopher. Young Mill read Latin and Greek authors at the age of eight, and at the age of thirteen studied Adam Smith and David Ricardo. After some years working for the East India Company he returned to England in 1850 and a year later he married Harriet Hardy. Among his works his *Systems of Logic* and *Principles of Political Economy* were written at 18 Kensington Square. His other works include the famous *Subjection of Women* (1869). He died in Avignon, in 1873.

MILLAIS, Sir John Everett (1829–96)

2 Palace Gate, W8

English painter, born in Southampton. Came to London in 1838 and he entered the Royal Academy. In 1848 he was associated with Holman Hunt and Dante Gabriel

Alfred
LORD MILNER
1854-1925
STATESMAN
lived here

Egypt. Chairman of the Board of the Inland Revenue 1892-7 and High Commissioner for South Africa 1879-1901. He was raised to the peerage as Baron Milner of St James and after the conclusion of the Boer War in 1902 was created a viscount. During the First World War he was a member of Lloyd-George's war cabinet. He died at Sturry Court, near Canterbury.

MILTON, John (1608–74)

St Mary-le-Bow Church, EC2

Poet, born in Bread Street, Cheapside, the son of a scrivener. Educated at St Paul's School and Christ's College, Cambridge. He spent seven years at Cambridge, during which he wrote 'On the morning of Christ's nativity', and then six years at Horton in preparation for his poetic vocation. It was at Horton that he wrote *L'Allegro, Il Penseroso, Comus,* and *Lycidas.* In 1643 he married Mary Powell, the daughter of a royalist, by whom he had three daughters. He was a formidable champion of the

Venezuelan patriot, born in Caracas, the son of wealthy parents. When he was 21 he sailed for Europe and joined the Spanish Army, being sent to Cuba, whence he fled to the United States. There he met George Washington. Then he travelled through Europe and joined France's revolutionary forces. Miranda lived in London for many years before returning to Venezuela, where he took command of the patriot army. Eventually he was defeated by the royalists, arrested, and sent to prison in La Carraca, Spain, where he died. He is known as 'El Precursor'.

MONDRIAN, Piet Cornelis (1872–1944)

60 Parkhill Road, NW3

Dutch artist, born in Amersfoort. After attending the Amsterdam Academy of Fine Arts for three years, he moved to Paris in 1910 and there came under the influence of the

parliamentary cause and his powers as a controversialist are seen in the many pamphlets he produced, ranging from *The Doctrine and Discipline of Divorce* (1643) to *Areopagitica: A Speech for the Liberty of Unlicensed Printing* (1644). His wife died in 1652 and Milton then married Catherine Woodcock. On her death he married again, this time Elizabeth Minshull. By now he was completely blind and in 1658 began to compose by dictation *Paradise Lost*, published in 1667. *Paradise Regained*, together with *Samson Agonistes*, appeared in 1671.

MIRANDA, Francisco de (1750–1816)

58 Grafton Way, W1

French Cubists. In 1914, with his compatriot van Doesburg, he founded the De Stijl movement of painters and architects. He came to London at the outbreak of the Second World War, and from thence to the United States. He died in New York.

MONTEFIORE, Sir Moses (1784–1885)

99 Park Lane, W1

Philanthropist and Jewish leader, lived here for sixty years.

MORDEN, John (1548–1623)

Hendon Senior High School, The Crest, NW4

English cartographer, born in Somerset. He travelled extensively throughout England and Wales, making topographical descriptions of the whole country as official mapmaker for Queen Elizabeth I. His

Speculum Britannia was published in 1596. His printed maps were the earliest to show existing roads.

MORE, Sir Thomas (1478–1535)

Cheyne Walk, SW3

English statesman, born in Milk Street, London, the son of a judge. Educated at St Anthony's School and at Canterbury Hall, Oxford. He was admitted to Lincoln's Inn in 1496 and sat in Parliament in 1504. A year later he married June Colt. She died in 1511 and within a month he married Alice Nuddleton, a widow. Moore's *Utopia*, published in Latin in

1516, is a satire on government and society. He was appointed Chancellor of the Duchy of Lancaster in 1525 and four years later was raised to the Chancellorship. Henry VIII counted upon More's support on the matter of his divorce from Queen Catherine, which would have enabled him to marry Anne Boleyn. But the Chancellor remained inflexible, and although his resignation was accepted by the king in 1532, he was indicted for high treason and beheaded on Tower Hill on 7 July 1535. He was canonized 400 years later, in 1935.

MORRELL, Lady Ottoline (1873–1938)

10 Gower Street, WC1

Literary hostess and patron of the arts, lived here.

MORRIS, William (1834–96)

Red House Lane, Bexley Heath

Poet, artist, and craftsman, born at Walthamstow. Educated at Marlborough School and Exeter College, Oxford. Studied to become an architect, then turned to painting before joining a decorating firm where he met D.G. Rossetti and Edward Burne-Jones. One of the founders of the *Oxford and Cambridge Magazine*. His *The Defence of Guenevere and Other Poems* was published in 1858. He also published verse translations of Virgil's *Aeneid* (1875) and Homer's *Odyssey* (1887), as well as prose romances such as *The House of the Wolfings* (1889). His socialist views found expression in *The Dream of John Ball* (1888) and *News from Nowhere* (1891). Morris founded the Kelmscott Press in 1890 and was a leading figure in the arts and crafts movement. Red House was built in 1859–60 by the architect Philip Webb for Morris, who lived here from 1860 to 1865.

MORRISON, Herbert Stanley, Baron Morrison of Lambeth (1888–1965)

55 Archery Road, SE9

Statesman and leader of the London County Council, lived here from 1929 to 1960.

MORSE, Samuel Finley Breese (1791–1872)

143 Cleveland Street, W1

American artist and inventor, born in Charleston, Mass. Educated at Yale. He came to England, where he studied historical painting from 1811 to 1815. On his return to the United States, he became a leading founder and first president of the National Academy of Design. He started to build telegraph models in 1837, invented the Morse Code a year later, and in 1843 built the first telegraphic line in the USA from Baltimore to Washington. He died in New York.

MOZART, Wolfgang Amadeus Chrysostom (1756–91)

180 Ebury Street, SW1

Austrian composer, born in Salzburg. Educated by his father, also a composer. At the age of five he played minuets and composed little pieces. He travelled throughout Europe with his family, residing in London from April 1764 to July 1765. Here he played for George III and Queen Charlotte. He composed symphonies, masses, and oratorios, and also well-known operas such as *Don Giovanni, The Magic Flute* and *Cosi Fan Tutte*. He died at the age of thirty-five, having written over 600 compositions.

MUNNINGS, Sir Alfred (1878–1959)

96 Chelsea Park Gardens, SW3

Painter and president of the Royal Academy (1944–9), lived here from 1929 to 1959.

N

NABUCO, Joaquim (1849–1910)

52 Cornwall Gardens, SW7

Brazilian statesman and diplomat. The scion of an old aristocratic family, he was appointed Brazilian Ambassador to London, being the last to be received as such by Queen Victoria. He campaigned for the abolition of slavery in Brazil, which finally came about in 1888.

NAPOLEON, Charles Louis Napoleon Bonaparte (1808–78)

1e King Street, SW1

Born in Paris, the third son of Louis Bonaparte, who was named King of Holland by his brother, Napoleon I.

Exiled in London on two occasions, during his second exile he was elected by four French *départements*, but did not accept the seats. On 10 December 1848, he was elected President of the French Republic, and in 1852 proclaimed Emperor of the French as Napoleon III. In July 1870 he declared war on Prussia. The French Army was defeated at Sedan, the emperor was taken prisoner and deposed. He settled with the ex-Empress Eugénie at Chislehurst in March 1871, living there until his death.

NELSON, Horatio, Viscount Nelson (1758–1805)

147 New Bond Street, W1

English sailor and naval hero, born at Burnham Thorpe, Norfolk. Entered the navy at the age of twelve on 1770 and served in the West Indies and on an Arctic expedition. Returning to the West Indies he married Frances Nesbit, a widow, in 1787. Remained without employment until 1793, when he took command of the *Agamemnon* and accompanied Lord Hood to the Mediterranean. It was in Naples that he first met Sir William and Lady Hamilton, in August 1793. During the battle for Corsica Nelson lost the sight of his right eye. After the Battle of Cape St Vincent in February 1797 he was promoted to rear-admiral. In July of that year he lost his right arm in action at Santa Cruz. After virtually destroying the French fleet in Aboukir Bay he was created Baron Nelson of the Nile. In November 1800 he parted from his wife. Nelson was also victorious at the Battle of Copenhagen in 1801, as a result of which he was created

Viscount Nelson. In 1803 he was appointed again to the Mediterranean and kept watch on the French Fleet at Toulon for two years. On 21 October 1805 he engaged the Franco-Spanish fleet under Villeneuve off Cape Trafalgar. The enemy were defeated but Nelson died of a musket shot before the victory was complete. He is buried in St Paul's Cathedral.

NEWMAN, John Henry, Cardinal (1801–90)

Old Broad Street, EC2

English theologian. Born in London, the son of a banker and a mother whose Calvinist views strongly influenced his early religious thinking. Went up to Trinity College, Oxford, in 1817 and became a fellow of Oriel in 1822. Curate of St Clement's, Oxford, in 1824. At Oriel he met Richard Hurrel Froude, with whom he toured the Mediterranean 1832–4. By 1830 Newman had broken with the Evangelicalism of his childhood and before long he was

a leading member of the Anglo-Catholic Oxford Movement. It was Newman who was responsible for the famous Tract 90 (1841) of *Tracts for the Times* in which he maintained that the intention of the Thirty-nine Articles was Catholic in essence. He was received into the Roman Church in 1845 and ordained a priest in Rome the following year. His works include *Lyra Apostolica* (1834) and *Apologia pro Vita Sua* (1864). Created a cardinal in 1879. He died in Birmingham and is buried in Rome.

NEWTON, Sir Isaac (1642–1727)

87 Jermyn Street, SW1

Scientist and mathematician, born at Woolsthorpe, Lincolnshire. Educated at Grantham Grammar School and at Trinity College, Cambrige, of which he became a fellow in 1667. Two years later he became Lucasian Professor of Mathematics at Cambridge and a Fellow of the Royal Society in 1672. It was during his absence from Cambridge in the plague years of 1655 to 1666 that he conceived the idea of universal gravitation as a result of considering the fall of an apple. After his fellowship of Trinity he turned his attention to optics and the construction of telescopes. By 1684 he had completed his theory of gravitation, expounded in detail in his great work *Philosophiae Naturalis Principia Mathematica* (1687), known generally as the *Principia*. He was knighted by Queen Anne on her visit to Cambridge in 1705. Newton was also an avid student of alchemy. He is buried in Westminster Abbey.

NIGHTINGALE, Florence (1820–1910)

10 South Street, W1

Nursing pioneer, born in Florence,

FLORENCE NIGHTINGALE
LEFT HER HOSPITAL ON THIS SITE FOR
THE CRIMEA ◆ OCTOBER 21ˢᵀ 1854

daughter of William Nightingale of Embly Park, Hampshire. Her family opposed her firm desire to become a nurse, then a disreputable occupation, but she persisted in her intentions and trained at Kaiserwerth (1851) and in Paris. After the Battle of the Alma she offered to go to the Crimea and organize nursing facilities at Scutari. Soon after her arrival, with 38 nurses, the hospital was overwhelmed by the arrival of the wounded from the Battle of Inkermann. She now had 10,000 men under her care and had to work in appalling conditions. Against all the odds she brought order out of chaos and returned to England in 1856 a national heroine. She devoted much of her life on her return to improving sanitary conditions in the army and to public health in India. She was awarded the Order of Merit in 1907. Her *Notes on Nursing* was published in 1859 and went through many editions. She is buried at East Wellow, near Romsey.

NOLLEKENS, Joseph (1737–1823)

44 Mortimer Street, W1

Sculptor, born in London, the son of a Belgian painter. At the age of thirteen he entered the studio of the sculptor Peter Scheemakers. After ten years in Rome he returned to England, established his studio in London. He became an associate of the Royal Academy in 1771 and a full member in 1772. After executing a bust of George III he became the most fashionable sculptor of his day,

his sitters including Dr Johnson, Sterne, Goldsmith, and Garrick. He died in London.

NOVELLO, Ivor (Ivor Novello Davies, 1893–1951)

11 Aldwych, WC2

Composer and actor, born in Cardiff, the son of Dame Clara Novello. Educated at Magdalen College School, Oxford where he was a chorister. Novello's most famous songs were those composed at the outbreak of the First World War, such as 'Keep the Home Fires Burning'. From 1921 he began to appear regularly on the London stage and

wrote several popular musicals, such as *Glamorous Night* (1935) and *The Dancing Years* (1939).

O

OATES, Laurence Edward Grace (1880–1912)

309 Upper Richmond Road, SW15

English explorer, born in Putney, educated at Eton. Saw service during the South African War and afterwards sailed on board the *Terranova* with the Scott expedition to the Antarctic. He reached the Pole with four of his comrades on 7 January 1912. On their return trip, with his hands and feet severely frostbitten, he thought his three remaining comrades had a better chance of survival without him, so he left their tent saying: 'I am just going outside, maybe for some time'.

Unfortunately, his sacrifice did no good to Scott and his comrades. Their bodies were found some months later.

OBRADOVICH, Dositey (1742–1811)

27 Clements Lane, EC4

A Serbian monk who fled his country and travelled through Europe, trying to win support for the cause of his country's independence. He spent some time in London. Eventually he was appointed Minister of Education of Serbia and founded a number of schools; he is considered as the father of modern Serbian Literature. He wrote his autobiography under the title *Life and Adventures*, published in two parts (1783, 1788).

ONSLOW, Arthur (1691–1768)

20 Soho Square, W1

British politician. He was Speaker of the House of Commons for thirty three years and was known for his independence and impartiality. He lived in Soho Square for nineteen years, and after his retirement moved to Great Russell Street, where he died.

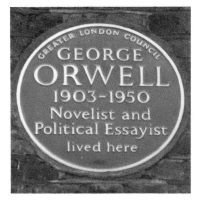

ORWELL, George (pseudonym of Eric Arthur Blair, 1903–50)

50 Lawford Road, NW5

English novelist and essayist, born in Motihari, Bengal, and educated as a King's Scholar at Eton. Served in the Indian Imperial Police in Burma from 1922 to 1927 (see his novel *Burmese Days*, 1935). Returning to Europe he lived in poverty, described in his book *Down and Out in Paris and*

London (1933). He fought on the Republican side in the Spanish Civil War and was wounded. *Homage to Catalonia* (1938) is the record of his war experiences. Considering himself to be a democratic socialist he became more and more critical of communism and totalitarianism. His two famous political satires, *Animal Farm* and *Nineteen Eighty-Four*, were published in 1945 and 1949 respectively. His other works include *Keep the Aspidistra Flying* (1936), *Coming Up for Air* (1939), and *The Road to Wigan Pier* (1937). He died in London.

27b Canonbury Square, N1

Orwell lived here.

P

PALMERSTON, Henry John Temple, 3rd Viscount (1784–1865)

Naval and Military Club, 94 Piccadilly, W1

English statesman, born at Broadlands, near Romsey, Hampshire. Educated at Harrow, Edinburgh, and St John's College, Cambridge. Succeeded to the peerage in 1802 and entered Parliament as Tory MP for Newport, Isle of Wight, in 1807. Secretary-at-War, 1809, and retained this position through successive administrations until 1828. A supporter of Catholic emancipation and became Foreign Secretary in Lord Grey's administration in 1830, a post he continued to hold, except for a break of four months during Peel's administration, for eleven years. Home Secretary in Lord Aberdeen's ministry of 1852. Became prime minister towards the end of the Crimean campaign. Lord Palmerston is buried in Westminster Abbey.

PARKINSON, James (1755–1824)

1 Hoxton Square, N1

Physician, famous for his research on *paralysis agitans*, today known as Parkinson's Disease. He was a radical in politics and is also remembered as a geologist, mainly as the author of *Organic Remains of a Former World*. He died in London.

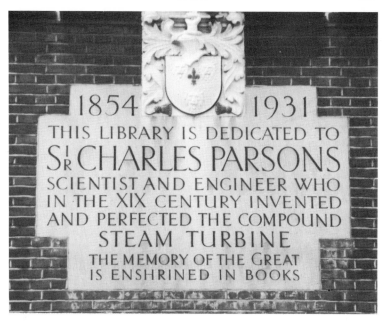

PARSONS, Sir Charles Algernon (1854–1931)

1 Guildford Street, WC1

Scientist and engineer, born in London, the fourth son of the 3rd Earl of Rosse. Educated privately and at St John's College, Cambridge. He joined the Armstrong Works in 1877 and in 1884 he entered into partnership with Messrs Clarke Chapman and Co. Five years later he established his own works at Heaton, Newcastle-upon-Tyne, for the manufacture of steam turbines, dynamos, and other electrical apparatus. His invention of the Parsons steam turbine, widely used in electric generating stations and for marine propulsion, brought him fame. He was made a Fellow of the Royal Society in 1898 and created Knight Commander of the Bath in 1911. He received the Order of Merit in 1927. Sir Charles Parsons died at Kingston, Jamaica, on board the *Duchess of Richmond*.

PATEL, Sardar Vallabhbhai Javerbhai (1875–1950)

23 Aldridge Villas, W11

Indian statesman, lived here.

PAVLOVA, Anna (1885–1931)

Ivy House, North End Road, NW11

Russian ballerina, born in St Petersburg. She studied at the Russian Imperial Ballet School, graduating as soloist in 1899; seven years later she was named prima ballerina. She appeared with great success at the Palace Theatre, London, with Mikhail Mordkin as her partner. After becoming the world's most famous prima ballerina, she settled in London with her husband and manager, Victor Dandré. Her most famous performances were in *Griselle, The Dying Swan, Don Quixote*, and her own ballet *Autumn Leaves*. She bought Ivy House in 1912 and lived here for many years. Anna Pavlova died at the Hague in 1931.

PEABODY, George (1795–1869)

80 Eaton Square, SW1

American philanthropist, born in South Danvers, Mass. After a number of business trips to England, he settled in London and here he established the firm George Peabody & Company, dealing with foreign exchange and US securities. He amassed a huge fortune and spent most of it on the establishment of a number of charitable institutions in his native country. In 1862 he set up a Trust Fund for the construction of houses for workers. He died in London in 1869.

PEPYS, Samuel (1632–1703)

Salisbury Court, EC4

Admiralty official and diarist. Born in Salisbury Court, near St Bride's Churchyard, the son of a tailor. Educated at St Paul's School and Magdalene College, Cambridge. Married Elizabeth Merchant in 1655. After the Restoration of Charles II, through the influence of his father's cousin, the Earl of Sandwich (formerly Sir Edward Montagu), he rose rapidly in the naval

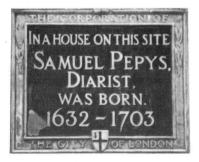

administration, becoming secretary to the Admiralty in 1672. He was accused of complicity in the Popish Plot of 1679 and lost his office but was reappointed in 1684. That same year he became president of the Royal Society. He was once again removed from office at the Revolution and he thereafter lived in retirement. His famous Diary runs from 1 January 1660 to 31 May 1669 (the year his wife died). It was written in cipher and remained in manuscript at Magdalene until 1825, when it was deciphered by John Smith and edited by Lord Braybrooke.

12–14 Buckingham Street, WC2

Site of the Navy Office where Pepys worked. Destroyed by fire in 1673.

PETRIE, Sir William Matthew Flinders (1853–1942)

5 Cannon Place, NW3

British egyptologist, born at Charlton, Kent. His early work was on Stonehenge published in 1880. He then devoted himself to Egyptian archaeology. In 1891 he discovered the ancient temple at Medum. Two years later he was appointed professor of Egyptology at University College, London and founded what is now the British School of Archaeology. He was knighted in 1923 and died in Jerusalem.

PINERO, Sir Arthur Wing (1855–1934)

40 Devonshire Street, W1

English playwright, born in London. At the age of 19 he was engaged as an actor at Edinburgh's Theatre Royal. He came to London in 1876 to play at the Globe Theatre. His first successful play was *The Money Spinner*. He wrote a number of plays, but *The Second Mrs Tanqueray* was perhaps his greatest success. It opened in 1893, with Mrs Patrick Campbell and George Alexander in the leading roles. Pinero was

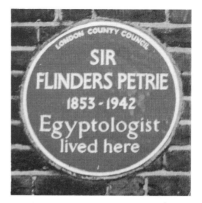

knighted in 1909. His other plays included *The Gay Lord Quex* (1899) and *His House in Order* (1906).

PITT, William, 1st Earl of Chatham (1708–78)

10 St James's Square, SW1

English statesman, born in Westminster. Educated at Eton and Trinity College, Oxford. Entered Parliament for Old Sarum in 1735. He took the side of Frederick, Prince of Wales, against the prince's father, George II. He was also an opponent of Walpole. He became Paymaster-General in 1746 but continual differences with the king led to his resignation in 1755. A year later he became secretary of state and virtual premier, whereupon he proceeded with his plans to carry on the war with France; but again he was forced to resign owing to the king's opposition. He left office in April 1757, only to be reinstated by public

opinion in June. He was now able to implement his war policy with brilliant effectiveness and a string of allied victories against the French resulted. He finally resigned from public service in 1768, though he continued to speak out on leading issues and was a strong critic of the government's belligerent attitude towards the American colonies. Pitt was the outstanding political orator of his age and on his death in May 1778 was given a public funeral and a statue in Westminster Abbey.

PITT, William (The Younger, 1759–1806)

120 Baker Street, W1

English statesman, second son of William Pitt, 1st Earl of Chatham, born at Hayes, near Bromley. Educated at Pembroke Hall, Cambridge. Called to the bar in 1780; entered Parliament as MP for Appleby in 1781. A year later he was

chancellor of the Exchequer, and in December 1783 became prime minister, at the age of twenty-five, though he had great difficulty in forming an administration. The general election of 1784 gave him an overwhelming majority and Pitt now had the power to form an administration that was to last for nearly twenty years. He introduced sweeping financial reforms, including the sinking fund for paying off the national debt. He attempted to maintain neutrality at the outbreak of the French Revolution but eventually war was declared in February 1793. After the Battle of Trafalgar in 1805 Pitt was hailed as the saviour of Europe, but the capitulation of Ulm and the Battle of Austerlitz broke his spirit and, already in ill health, he died in January 1806, his last words being 'Oh, my country! how I leave my country!' He was buried in Westminster Abbey.

PLACE, Francis (1771–1854)

21 Brompton Square, SW3

English reformer, born in London. He was apprenticed to a leather breeches maker and eventually opened his own tailor shop. A great admirer of Jeremy Bentham, Place opposed the Combination Laws forbidding trade unions. He was also a leading campaigner in the agitations that led to the passing of the Reform Bill in 1832 and he was a pioneer student of birth control. He died in London.

POMBAL, Sebastiao José de Carvalho e Mello, Marquess of (1699–1782)

23–4 Golden Square, W1

Portuguese statesman, born at Soure, near Coimbra. He was Portuguese Ambassador to London from 1739 to 1744. In 1749 he was appointed Secretary of State for War and

Foreign Affairs, organizing Portugal's education, finance, and armed forces. He expelled the Jesuits, built up new industries, promoted the development of the colonies, and reconstructed Lisbon after it was destroyed by earthquake in 1775. He was created a Marquess in 1770.

POPE, Alexander (1688–1744)

Plough Court, 32 Lombard Street, EC3

English poet, born the son of a Catholic linen-draper who settled at Binfield in Windsor Forest in the year of Pope's birth. Denied a formal education by his religion, Pope was precociously self-educated and through the offices of the elderly Restoration wit William Wycherley was introduced to London literary circles. His *Essay in Criticism* (1711) introduced him to Addison and his circle, whilst *Windsor Forest* (1713) brought him to the attention of the Tories and the friendship of Jonathan Swift. Pope, who was physically deformed as a result of childhood illness, was a member of the Scriblerus Club which included leading writers such as Swift, John Gay, and Arbuthnot. His genius for satire was shown in 1712 by *The Rape of the Lock*, whilst his lyric gifts were demonstrated by the 'Epistle of Eloisa to Abelard' and 'Elegy to the Memory of an Unfortunate Lady', which both appeared in his *Works* (1717). That same year Pope's father died and he moved with his mother to Twickenham. *The Dunciad*, a devastating satire on contemporary dullards in literature, appeared in 1728 (enlarged edition 1729). Pope also wrote philosophical and moral meditations such as *An Essay on Man* (1733–4) and *Moral Essays* (1731–5), as well as transactions of the *Iliad* and the *Odyssey*. He is buried in Twickenham Church.

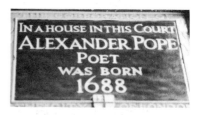

R

RAFFLES, Sir Thomas Stamford (1781–1826)

Highwood House, Mill Hill, NW7

English colonial administrator, born on board a merchant ship commanded by his father off Port Morant, Jamaica. Entered the service of the East India Company and in 1805 took up an appointment in Penang. As secretary to Lord Minto he was involved in the expedition against Java, of which he became lieutenant-governor in 1811, a post he held until Java was returned to the Dutch in 1815. Returned to England owing to ill health in 1816 and the following year published his *History of Java* and was knighted.

From 1818 he lived chiefly in Bencoolen as its governor and in 1819 persuaded the company to acquire the island of Singapore. He returned to England in 1824 but the ship carrying his immense collection of papers and zoological and botanical collections caught fire off Sumatra. Lived in retirement here for the rest of his life and was first president of the Zoological Society of London, which he helped to found.

RAGLAN, Fitzroy James Henry Somerset, 1st Baron (1788–1855)

5 Stanhope Gate W1

British general, born at Badminton,

Gloucestershire, the youngest son of the 5th Duke of Beaufort. Educated at Westminster School. He entered the Army in 1804 and served on the staff of Sir Arthur Wellesley (later, 1st Duke of Wellington) in the expedition to Copenhagen. He remained with him, first as aide-de-camp and then as military secretary when the duke went to Portugal and Spain. Raglan saw action at Badajoz. He married Emily Harriet, Wellington's niece. He lost his right arm at the Battle of Waterloo. Elevated to the peerage in 1852 and promoted to field-marshal in 1854. Led the expeditionary force to the Crimea, for the disasters of which Raglan was an undeserved scapegoat.

RAMMOHUN ROY (1774–1833)

49 Bedford Square, WC1

Indian scholar and religious reformer, lived here.

RATHBONE, Eleanor (1872–1946)

Tufton Court, Tufton Street, SW1

Pioneer of family allowances, lived here.

READING, Rufus Daniel Isaacs, 1st Marquess of (1860–1935)

32 Curzon Street, W1

Lawyer and statesman, born in London, the son of a merchant. Educated at University College, London and overseas. Called to the bar in 1887. Liberal MP for Reading 1904, solicitor-general 1910, and later attorney-general. Isaacs was accused of corruption during the Marconi affair, his brother being manager director of the company, but was aquitted by a special committee of the House of Commons. As Lord Chief Justice, he presided over Sir Roger Casement's trial. British ambassador in Washington from 1918 to 1921 and

Viceroy of India from 1921 to 1926. He was created a peer in 1914 as Baron Reading of Erleigh and in 1926 he was created Marquess, the first commoner to be so elevated since the Duke of Wellington.

RESCHID PASHA, Mustapha (1800–58)

1 Bryanston Square, W1

Turkish politician and diplomat, ambassador to France and England. Appointed Minister of Foreign Affairs, he eventually became Grand Vizir and as such he attempted to modernize his country, introducing political and social reforms. He also re-organized the army. Reschid was deeply hostile to Russia.

REYNOLDS, Sir Joshua (1723–92)

Fanum House, Leicester Square, WC2

English painter, born at Plympton Earls, near Plymouth, the son of a clergyman and schoolmaster. Showed an early talent in portraiture and was apprenticed to Thomas Hudson. Accompanied Commodore Keppel to the Mediterranean in 1749 and spent three years studying in Italy. He returned to London and by 1760 was established as the leading portrait painter of his day. Elected first president of the Royal Academy on its establishment in 1768 and was knighted the following year. Became the king's painter in 1784. In 1760 he moved from Great Newport Street to a house on this site, where he lived until his death. He is buried in the crypt of St Paul's Cathedral.

RIPON, George Frederick Samuel Robinson, Marquess of (1827–1909)

9 Chelsea Embankment, SW3

English statesman, born in London, only son of the 1st Earl of Ripon.

Entered Parliament for Hull in 1852
as an advanced Liberal, for
Huddersfield in 1853, and for the
West Riding of Yorkshire in 1857.
Two years later he succeeded to his
father's title, and then to that of his
uncle, the Earl de Grey. After
entering the House of Lords he was
appointed Under-secretary for War
(1859), then Under-secretary for
India (1861). In 1863 he was
appointed Secretary for War, with a
seat in cabinet. Three years later he
became Secretary for India. In
Gladstone's first administration he
was appointed Lord President of the
Council; he resigned in 1873, on
private grounds. He was created a
Marquess in 1871 and converted to
Roman Catholicism in 1874. On
Gladstone's return to power in 1880,
Lord Ripon was appointed Viceroy
of India, a controversial appointment
due to his Catholicism. He became
First Lord of the Admiralty in 1886
and Colonial Secretary in 1892. He

died at Studley Royal, near Ripon.

RIZAL, José (1861–96)
37 Chalcot Crescent, NW1

Filipino patriot and writer, born in
Calambo in the Philippines.
Educated at the University of Manila
and in Madrid where he studied
medicine. His anti-Spanish views
found expression in two novels,
Noli me tangere (1886) and *El Fili
busterismo* (1891). At the outbreak
of the Philippine Revolution of 1896,
Rizal was on his way to Cuba for
medical service with the Spanish
Army. Arrested aboard ship, he was
brought back to Manila, where he
was found guilty of complicity,
sentenced to death, and executed by
a firing squad.

ROBERTS, Frederick Sleigh, Earl Roberts of Kandahar, Pretoria, and Waterford (1832–1914)
47 Portland Place, W1

British soldier, born in Cawnpore.
Educated at Eton, Sandhurst, and
Addiscombe. He obtained his first
commission in the Bengal Artillery in
1851. He saw action in India

WITHIN A FEW FEET OF THIS SPOT,
JOHN ROGERS,
JOHN BRADFORD,
JOHN PHILPOT,
AND OTHER
SERVANTS OF GOD,
SUFFERED DEATH BY FIRE
FOR THE FAITH OF CHRIST,
IN THE YEARS 1555, 56, 1557.

including the siege of Lucknow, and later in the Afghan War. He was awarded the VC in 1858. When Gen. James Primrose was besieged in Kandahar, after the total defeat of a British brigade at Maiwand, Roberts proceeded with 10,000 troops to march through Afghanistan to relieve the garrison, which he achieved with complete success. During the Boer War he took command of the British Forces, relieved Kimberley, and made the great advance to Pretoria. Created Earl in 1901 and died while inspecting troops in the field in France.

ROGERS, John (c. **1500–55)**

West Smithfield, EC1

Martyr, born near Birmingham. Educated at Pembroke Hall, Cambridge. In 1534 he went to Antwerp as chaplain to the English merchants. There he abandoned the Roman Catholic faith and married an Antwerp lady. He then returned to England and in 1551 he was made a prebendary of St Paul's. On the accession of Queen Mary, Rogers preached at St Paul's Cross against 'popery, idolatry and superstition'. Sentenced to death for heresy, he was burned at Smithfield, the first Protestant martyr of Mary's reign.

ROHMER, Sax (Arthur Sarsfield Ward, 1886–1959)

51 Herne Hill, SE24

The author of mystery stories and creator of Dr Fu Manchu lived here.

ROKESLEY, Gregory de (*d.* 1291)

72 Lombard Street, EC3

A wealthy merchant, Chief Master of the King's Mints. Rokesley was eight times Lord Mayor of London.

ROMNEY, George (1734−1802)

Holly Bush Hill, NW3

English painter, born at Dalton-in-Furness, Lancashire, the son of a cabinet maker. He came to London in 1762, leaving behind his wife and children, in order to dedicate himself to art. He went to Italy in 1773, staying there for two years. On his return to London he met Emma Hart (the future Lady Hamilton), who exercised a morbid fascination over the painter: he painted her face in over fifty paintings. In 1797, Romney moved to a large studio in Hampstead, but due to his declining health he returned to his wife, at Kendal, where he died.

RONALDS, Sir Francis (1788−1873)

Coach House, 26 Upper Mall, W6

British inventor, pioneer of the telegraph. In 1816 he invented a simple apparatus made of circular plates inscribed with letters and figures and electrically operated, now exhibited at the Science Museum, South Kensington. Superintendent of the Meteorological Observatory at Kew, 1843, Fellow of the Royal Society, 1844, knighted in 1871.

ROSEBERY, Archibald Philip Primrose, 5th Earl of (1847−1929)

20 Charles Street, W1

British statesman, born in London. Educated at Eton and Christ Church, Oxford. A member of the Liberal Party, he was appointed Secretary of Foreign Affairs in two Gladstone

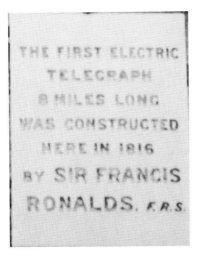

governments, in 1886 and 1892. He became Liberal premier on Gladstone's retirement in 1894. Defeated in the election of 1895 he remained leader of the Liberal opposition until 1896. Created Earl of Midlothian in 1911 and First Chairman of the London County Council.

Ross, Sir James Clark (1800–62)

2 Eliot Place, SE3

Polar explorer, born in London. Entered the Royal Navy in 1812. Ross accompanied his uncle, Sir John Ross, on his Arctic expeditions, reaching the North Magnetic Pole in 1831. He also accompanied Sir W.E. Parry on his four Arctic expeditions (1819–27). He commanded HMS *Erbus* and *Terror* during the Antarctic expedition from 1839 to 1843, discovering the Ross Sea. He published *Voyage of Discovery . . . in the Southern and Antarctic Regions* in 1847, and one year later he was elected a Fellow of the Royal Society. He died in Aylesbury.

Ross, Sir Ronald (1857–1932)

18 Cavendish Square, W1

Physician and medical researcher, born at Almora, India. Studied medicine at St Bartholomew's

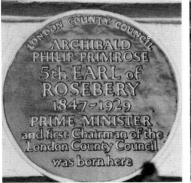

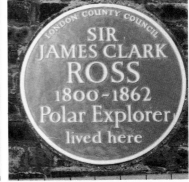

Hospital and qualified in 1881. Served in the Indian Medical Service until 1899. His interest in tropical diseases led him to the discovery that malaria was transmitted by Anophelin mosquitoes. He was appointed professor of tropical medicine at the University of Liverpool. Ross was awarded the Nobel Prize for Medicine (1902) and was created KCB in 1911. In 1926 the Ross Institute was founded in his honour and he was appointed Chief Director.

ROSSETTI, Dante Gabriel (1828–82)

110 Hallam Street, W1

Poet and painter, brother to the poet Christina Rossetti and the critic William Michael Rossetti. Born in London, educated at King's College School and the Royal Academy Antique School. With Millais and Holman Hunt, in 1848, he formed the Pre-Raphaelite Brotherhood, dedicated to opposing modern art forms and returning to pre-Renaissance techniques and approaches. Rossetti's most celebrated paintings include *The Annunciation* (1850), *The Blue Closet* (1857), *Beata Beatrix* (*c.* 1863), *The Beloved* (1865), *Prosperine* (1874), and *The Wedding of St George and the Princess Sabra* (1857). His model for many of his greatest works was Elizabeth Siddal, whom he married in 1860. She died two years later and in his grief Rossetti enclosed the manuscripts of his poems in her coffin. These were disinterred seven years later and published. His poetical works include *Ballads and Sonnets* (1881), as well as translations from French, German, and Italian.

17 Red Lion Square, WC1

Rossetti lived here, as did William Morris (q.v.) and Edward Burne-Jones.

ROWLANDSON, Thomas (1757–1827)

16 John Adam Street, WC2

Artist and caricaturist, born in Old
Jewry, London, the son of a City
merchant. He studied at the Royal
Academy, and then in Paris. His work
vigorously chronicles the life of his
time and he was the creator of the
famous 'Dr Syntax' as well as the
illustrator of Sterne's *Sentimental
Journey*.

RUSSELL, Edward, Earl of Orford (1653–1727)

43 King Street, WC2

English Admiral, the youngest son of
the 4th Earl of Orford. Commanded
the Anglo-Dutch fleet of 99 ships
which engaged the French off the
Normandy coast in May 1692. The
French Fleet, commanded by
Tourville, had received orders from
King Louis XIV to protect the

crossing of a mixed French and Irish
Army to invade England. Despite a
courageous fight by Tourville, Russell
won an overwhelming victory which
forced Louis XIV to sue for peace.
The operation was known as the
Battle of La Hogue.

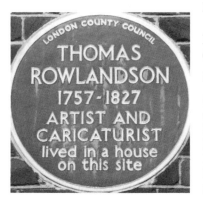

RUSSELL, John, 1st Earl (1792–1878)

37 Chesham Place, SW1

Statesman, born in London, the third
son of the 6th Duke of Bedford.
Educated at the University of
Edinburgh. Entered Parliament in
1813 as the member for Tavistock.
Paymaster of the forces in Earl Grey's
ministry and one of the framers of

the Reform Bill of 1832. Prime minister 1846–52 and again in 1865. Created Earl Russell in 1861. Died at Pembroke Lodge, Richmond Park.

RUTHERFORD, Mark (pseudonym of William Hale White, 1831–1913)

19 Park Hill, Carshalton

Writer, born in Bedford. Qualified as a Congregational minister but turned to journalism and writing. Translated Spinoza's *Ethica* (1883). Author of *The Autobiography of Mark Rutherford* (1881) and its sequel *Mark Rutherford's Deliverance* (1885). Also wrote *The Revolution in Tanner's Lane* (1887) and *Miriam's Schooling* (1890). Lived here.

S

ST THOMAS À BECKET
(?1118–70)
86 Cheapside, EC2

Archbishop of Canterbury and
martyr, born in London, the son of a
wealthy Norman immigrant.
Educated at Merton Priory, London,
and Paris. He entered the service of
Archbishop Theobald of Canterbury
in 1142, became Archdeacon of
Canterbury in 1154, and that same
year was appointed Henry II's
Chancellor. Elected Archbishop of
Canterbury in 1162, his relations
with the king deteriorated rapidly,
and eventually he was forced to flee
to France in 1164. On his return to
England, he was murdered by four
knights in Canterbury Cathedral. He
was canonized in 1173.

SAN MARTIN, José de
(1778–1850) (NW8)
23 Park Road, W8

South American patriot, born in
Yapeyú, Argentina, the son of an
aristocratic Spanish family. He served
for 22 years in the Spanish Army,
attaining the rank of lieutenant-
colonel, and saw action in the siege
of Oran and at the Battle of Bailen,
where the Spanish General Castanos
defeated the French army under
General Dupont. Back in Argentina,
San Martin organized the Republican
army and after a long struggle
defeated the Spaniards at Chacabuco
and Maipu, liberating Argentina and
Chile, though he failed to liberate

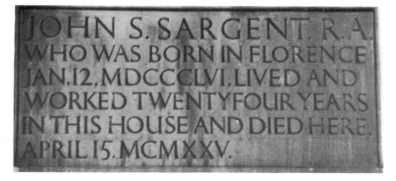

JOHN S. SARGENT. R.A.
WHO WAS BORN IN FLORENCE
JAN. 12, MDCCCLVI, LIVED AND
WORKED TWENTYFOUR YEARS
IN THIS HOUSE AND DIED HERE.
APRIL 15. MCMXXV.

Peru. He died, self-exiled, in
Boulogne-Sur-Mer and is buried
in the Cathedral of Buenos Aires,
Argentina.

**SARGENT, John Singer
(1856–1925)**
31 Tite Street, SW3

American painter, born in Florence of
American parents. He studied art in
the Paris studio of Carolus Duran and
at the Ecole des Beaux Arts. He went
to Madrid to study the works of the
Spanish masters, particularly
Velazquez. He eventually settled in
London where he soon became the
most fashionable portrait painter of his
time. He died in London and is buried
in Brookwood Cemetery, Surrey.

**SAVARKAR, Vinayak Damodar
(1883–1966)**
65 Cromwell Avenue, Highgate, N6

Indian patriot and philanthropist, lived
here.

SCOTT, Robert Falcon (1868–1912)
56 Oakley Street, SW3

English Antarctic explorer, born near
Davenport. Educated at Stoke
Damerel and at Stubbington House,
Fareham. He entered the Royal Navy
in 1881, on HMS *Britannia*,
becoming a midshipman two years
later. In 1900 he became commander
of the National Antarctic Expedition
on HMS *Discovery*, exploring the
Ross Sea and discovering Edward VII
Land. He was promoted to captain in
1906 and four years later undertook a
second expedition to the Antarctic,

this time in the *Terra Nova*. With a party that included Captain Laurence Oates (see p. 112) he reached the South Pole on 17 January 1912, only to find that Amundsen had preceded them by a month. The return journey turned into tragedy. On 17 February Petty Officer Evans died, and a month later Oates walked out of their tent, hoping to save his comrades. On 12 November, a search party found the bodies of Captain Scott, Dr Wilson, and Lt. Bowers, as well as Scott's records and diaries, now in the British Library. The Scott Polar Research Institute in Cambridge was founded in his memory.

SEFERIS (real name: Seferiades), George (1900–71)

7 Sloane Avenue, SW3

Greek poet who won the Nobel Prize for Literature in 1963. His first visit to London was in 1924, as a student.

Then, from 1931 to 1934, he returned as Greek Consul. After the Second World War he was appointed Greek Ambassador to London.

SHACKLETON, Sir Ernest Henry (1874–1922)

12 Westwood Hill, SE26

Born in Kilkee, Ireland. Educated at Dulwich College. He entered the merchant navy with the White Star Shipping Line and was a junior officer under Captain Scott (see p. 132) on HMS *Discovery*. After taking part in other expeditions he returned to Antarctica in 1909 as leader of the British Antarctic Expedition. He led a party which reached within 97 miles of the South Pole. On his return he was knighted and made a CVO. In March 1914 he left England leading the British Imperial Trans-Antarctic Expedition. His ship, HMS *Endeavour*, was crushed by pack ice. The crew

reached Elephant Island after drifting for five months. Shackleton and five others sailed 800 miles to South Georgia in a whale boat and eventually organized a rescue for his men. He died in South Georgia while on a third voyage to Antarctica.

SHARP, Cecil James (1859–1924)

4 Maresfield Gardens, NW3

Collector of English folk songs and dances, lived here.

SHAW, George Bernard (1856–1950)

29 Fitzroy Square, W1

Dramatist, critic, and essayist, born in Dublin of Irish Protestant parents. In 1871 he entered a firm of land agents but left Ireland for good in 1876. In London he struggled to establish himself as a writer and journalist, writing for the *Pall Mall Gazette*, *The World*, and *The Saturday Review*. Between 1879 and 1883 he wrote five novels, including *Love Among the Artists* and *Cashel Byron's Profession*. From 1884 to 1911 he was a key member of the Fabian Society, for which he edited *Fabian Essays* (1889) and produced several popular socialist tracts. In 1898 he married the Irish heiress Charlotte Payne-Townsend, after which he devoted himself mainly to writing plays. His prodigious output includes such classics as *Man and Superman* (1903), *Back to Methuselah* (1921), *Saint Joan* (1924), *Arms and the Man*, *Mrs Warren's Profession*, and *Major Barbara* (1907). Shaw's range of interests was wide, from vegetarianism to photography. He was awarded the Nobel Prize for Literature in 1925 and died at the age of ninety-four, at Ayot St Lawrence.

SHELLEY, Percy Bysshe (1792–1822)

3 Poland Street, W1

English poet, born at Field Place, Horsham, Sussex, educated at Eton, where he was bullied, and at University College, Oxford, from whence he was expelled (with his friend Thomas Jefferson Hogg) for writing and publishing a pamphlet called *The Necessity of Atheism*. The year of his expulsion (1811) he married Harriet Westbrook, aged sixteen, and the couple embarked on a wandering existence, with Shelley dedicated to 'reforming the world' and fired by the teachings of the philosopher William Godwin. In

GEORGE BERNARD SHAW
LIVED IN THIS HOUSE
FROM 1887 TO 1898

'FROM THE COFFERS OF HIS GENIUS
HE ENRICHED THE WORLD'

1814 Shelley left England with Godwin's daughter Mary, leaving Harriet behind. He married Mary after Harriet drowned herself in the Serpentine. *Alastor* was published in 1816, the year Shelley met Byron, who formed a liaison with Mary's half-sister, Claire Clairmont. The summer spent with Byron in Switzerland produced Shelley's 'Hymn to Intellectual Beauty' and 'Mont Blanc', whilst during the winter of 1816–17 he wrote 'Laon and Cythna' (later retitled 'The Revolt of Islam'). In 1818, beset by legal problems and the ever-present lack of money, Shelley and Mary left England for Italy. During the summer he wrote 'Lines Written in the Euganean Hills' and 'Julian and Maddalo'. His great verse drama *Prometheus Unbound* was published in 1820. At Pisa from the end of 1819 many of Shelley's finest lyrics were written, including 'Ode to the West Wind' and 'To a Skylark'. In 1821 the Shelleys moved to Lerici on the Gulf of Spezia. On 8 July 1822 Shelley was drowned while on his way by boat to meet Leigh Hunt and his family at Leghorn. His ashes are buried in the Protestant Cemetery at Rome.

SHERATON, Thomas (1751–1806)
163 Wardour Street, W1

English furniture designer, born at Stockton-on-Tees, the son of a cabinet-maker. He settled in London about 1790 and his neo-classical designs established him as a leading influence on contemporary furniture making. He published *The Cabinet Maker and Upholsterer's Drawing Book* in four parts, between 1791 and 1794.

SHERIDAN, Richard Brinsley (1751–1816)
10 Hertford Street, W1

Dramatist and politician, born in Dublin and educated at Harrow.

Formed an early romantic attachment to Elizabeth Linley, whom he married in 1773. The couple settled in London with little money and Sheridan set about establishing himself as a playwright. *The Rivals* was produced at Covent Garden in January 1775 and was a great success. The following year Sheridan acquired Garrick's share in the Drury Lane Theatre and there produced *The School for Scandal*, followed in 1779 by *The Critic*. In 1780 Sheridan was elected MP for Stafford and was under-secretary for foreign affairs in the Rockingham administration. During the impeachment of Warren Hastings in 1787 he first showed his brilliance as a parliamentary orator. His political career came to an end in 1812 and the following year he was arrested for debt. He died virtually penniless, having suffered in his last years from brain disease, and was given a public funeral. He is buried in Westminster Abbey.

SIMON, Sir John (1816–1904)

40 Kensington Square, W8

Pathologist and pioneer of public health, born in London, the son of a leading member of the London Stock Exchange. Educated at C.P. Burney's School, Greenwich. He then studied medicine with Joseph Henry Green at St Thomas's Hospital. In 1840 he became Assistant Surgeon to King's College Hospital, and seven years later he was made Surgeon and Lecturer on Pathology at St Thomas's. Appointed Medical Officer of Health to the City of London, and as such he dealt with the problems of water supply and sewage disposal.

SLOANE, Sir Hans, 1st Baronet (1660–1753)

4 Bloomsbury Place, WC1

Physician, born at Killyleagh, County Down, son of an Ulster Scot. After studying medicine in London

he went to France and took his MD degree. In 1687 he went to Jamaica as physician to the Duke of Albemarle's staff. There he collected about 800 new species of plants. In 1693 he became secretary to the Royal Society. He was created a baronet in 1716 and became president of the College of Physicians in 1719, then physician-general to the army (1722), physician to George I, and president of the Royal Society in 1727. On his death, he bequeathed his valuable library, manuscripts, and coin collections to the British Museum.

SMITH, Frederick Edwin, 1st Earl of Birkenhead (1872–1930)

32 Grosvenor Gardens, SW1

Lawyer and statesman, lived here.

SMITH, William Henry (1825–91)

12 Hyde Park Street, W2

Newsagent, bookseller, and statesman, born in London. His father was the founder of W.H. Smith & Son, in the Strand, and William became a partner at an early age. After contesting unsuccessfully for Westminster in 1865, Smith won the seat in 1868. He was secretary to the Treasury in 1874, first lord of the Admiralty in 1877, secretary for war in 1885, chief secretary for Ireland in 1885, and again secretary for war in 1886. He died at Walmer Castle and his widow received a Peerage in her own right as Viscountess Hambleden.

SMITH, Sydney (1771–1845)

14 John Street, WC1

Author, clergyman, and wit, born at Woodford, Essex, educated at Winchester and New College, Oxford. Ordained in 1796. Married Catharine Pybus in 1800 and settled in Edinburgh, where he was a co-founder of the *Edinburgh Review*.

gravitated a number of leading French *emigres*, including Talleyrand (see p. 142). She was allowed to return to Paris by Napoleon in 1797 and in 1800 she published her celebrated *Literature et ses rapports avec les institutions sociales. De l'Allemagne*, which introduced German literary and philosophical ideas to the French reading public, appeared in 1810. The first impression was seized by the censor and destroyed and Madame de Staël herself was exiled as a result. Her other works include two novels, *Delphine* (1802) and *Corinne* (1807). She died in Paris in July 1817.

His *Peter Plymley's Letters*, first published in the *Edinburgh Review* and written in favour of Catholic emancipation, appeared in 1807. He held livings in Yorkshire and then Somerset and in 1831 was made a canon of St Paul's. He was a brilliant wit and conversationalist.

STAËL, Anne Louise Germaine Necker, Madame de (1766–1817)

Argyll Street, W1
(rear of Dickins and Jones)

French writer, daughter of Jacques Necker, the French minister of finance. In 1785 she married Baron de Staël-Holstein, Swedish ambassador in Paris, from whom she separated in 1798. Before the outbreak of the French Revolution Madame de Staël's salon was the most brilliant in Paris. She left Paris for Coppet in September 1792 and then settled in England, at Mickleham in Surrey, and to her side

STANHOPE, Charles, 3rd Earl (1735–1816)

20 Mansfield Street, W1

Reformer and inventor, born in London. Educated at Eton and Geneva. Entered parliament as MP for Chipping Wycombe in 1780 and

retained his seat until 1786 when he succeeded to the peerage. Married Lady Hester, sister of the second William Pitt, in 1774. He sympathized with the French Revolution and liked to call himself 'Citizen Stanhope'. He invented the printing press and microscopic lens bearing his name, two calculating machines, and a new kind of cement. He died at Chevening.

STEPHENSON, Robert (1803–59)

35 Gloucester Square, W2

Engineer, son of George Stephenson, inventor of the steam locomotive. Born at Willington Quay, Northumberland. Educated at Bruce's Academy, Newcastle-upon-Tyne, and the University of Edinburgh. He assisted his father in surveying the Stockton and Darlington Railway and after three years in South America became manager of his father's locomotive works in Newcastle. Designed the Britannia Tubular Bridge (1850) and the High Level Bridge at Newcastle (1849). MP for Whitby from 1847 until his death.

STOKER, Abraham, known as Bram (1847–1912)

18 St Leonard's Terrace, SW3

Author of *Dracula*. Born in Dublin, educated at Trinity College. He settled in London, and he met Sir

Henry Irving, who retained him as his secretary and manager of the Lyceum Theatre. *Dracula* was published in 1895.

STRANG, William (1859–1921)

20 Hamilton Terrace, NW8

Scottish painter and illustrator, lived here from 1920 to 1921.

STUART, John McDouall (1815–66)

9 Campden Hill Square, W8

Explorer, born at Dysart, Fife. The first person to cross Australia from south to north. Mount Stuart is named after him. His book *Exploration in Australia* was published in 1864.

SUESS, Eduard (1831–1914)

4 Duncan Terrace, N1

Austrian geologist, born in London. Educated at the universities of Prague and Vienna, specializing in invertebrate paleontology. He was appointed professor of geology at the University of Vienna in 1857. He held this position until 1901. His masterpiece, *Das Anlitz der Erde*, published between 1885 and 1907, was translated into English as *The Face of the Earth*. Suess died in Vienna.

SUN YAT-SEN, or Sun Wen (1866–1925)

4 Gray's Inn Place, WC1

Called the Father of the Chinese Republic. Born at a farming village in the Kwantung Province. Educated at Honolulu and at the medical school in Hong Kong, where he took an MD in 1894. After China's defeat by Japan in 1895 he took part in a revolutionary plot, barely escaping execution. Self-exiled, he founded the Kuomintang, adopting what he called the 'Three Principles of the People': Nationalism, Democracy, and Socialism. The Ching Dinasty was overthrown in 1911 while Sun Yat-Sen was in London. He returned to

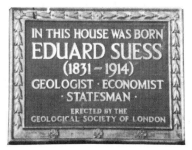

forty years to collecting data on rainfall. He founded the British Rainfall Organization, which after his death was integrated into the Meteorological Office. Symons was elected a Fellow of the Royal Society in 1878, and it was through his intervention that an inquiry was made into the Krakatoa eruption in 1883. He was twice elected president of the Royal Meteorological Society.

SZABO, Violette (1921–45)

18 Burnley Road, SW9

Secret agent, married to Etienne Szabo, an officer of the French Legion who was killed at the battle of El Alamein. She was sent to France by the Special Operations Executive to organize subversion, sabotage, and guerrilla warfare against the Germans. She was captured, tortured, and executed. Was posthumously awarded the George Cross and the Croix de Guerre.

China to become provisional president of the new republic. Six years later he was proclaimed President. He died in Peking, where he was trying to bring peace between northern and southern leaders.

SYMONS, George James (1838–1900)
62 Camden Square, NW1

British meteorologist, who dedicated

T

TAGORE, Sir Rabindranath (1861–1941)

3 Villas on the Heath, Vale of Health, NW3

Indian poet and philosopher, born in Calcutta, youngest son of Maharshi Devendranath, and grandson of Prince Dwarkanath Tagore. In 1877 he was sent to England to study law but returned to India, where in 1901 he established the Santiniketan, an unconventional school, at Bolpur. Tagore was awarded the Nobel Prize for Literature in 1913 and knighted in 1915. Many of his works have been translated into English, including *The Gardener, One Hundred Poems* of *Kabir, Broken Ties*, and *The Religion of Man*.

TALLEYRAND-PÉRIGORD, Charles Maurice de (1754–1838)

21 Hanover Square, W1

French statesman and diplomatist, born in Paris, the son of Lt General Charles Maurice de Talleyrand-Périgord. Educated at the Collège d'Harcourt and at St Sulpice. His uncle, the Archbishop of Rheims, appointed him vicar-general and in 1788 he was made Bishop of Autun. Later, as a representative of the Constituent Assembly, he proposed the confiscation of all Church

properties and the abolition of Feudalism. This led to his excommunication by Pope Pius VI. He was foreign minister both during the Consulate and under the Empire. As Ambassador to London in 1834 he contributed to the creation of Belgium as an independent nation. Talleyrand was a clever and intelligent politician who, after surviving the French Revolution, was able to serve the Empire and the Restoration.

TERRY, Dame Ellen Alice (1848–1928)

215 King's Road, SW3

Actress, born at Coventry, daughter of a provincial actor. She made her stage début at the age of sixteen at the Haymarket Theatre. A year later she married the painter G.F. Watts; the marriage was a failure but Watts refused her a divorce and later she eloped with Edward Godwin. She

returned to the stage for a brief period in 1867, playing with Henry Irving for the first time. After seven years' retirement she played Portia at the Prince of Wales's Theatre. Her second marriage to the actor E.A. Wardell also ended in divorce. When Henry Irving assumed the management of the Lyceum Theatre he engaged her as his leading lady, thus starting a long lasting and successful partnership. She was awarded the GBE in 1925. Dame Ellen Terry died at her house in Small Hythe, near Tenterden, Kent.

THACKERAY, William Makepeace (1811–63)

16 Young Street, W8

Novelist and journalist, born in Calcutta, where his father was a clerk in the East Indian Company. After his father's death Thackeray's mother married again and the boy was sent back to England to be educated at Charterhouse, and later at Trinity College, Cambridge. He left Cambridge without taking a degree, though he made useful friends in Edward FitzGerald, Tennyson, and others. He entered the Middle Temple in 1831 but soon abandoned his legal studies. Having spent much of his patrimony on foreign travel he tried to establish himself as a journalist writing for a variety of magazines under several pseudonyms, including Michael Angelo Titmarsh. He married Isabella Shawe in 1836 but parted from her in 1840 after the birth of their third child, an event which had deranged his wife's mind. Thackeray began contributing to *Punch* in 1842 and pieces such as 'Jeames's Diary' and 'The Snobs of England' (snobbery being one of Thackeray's great themes) brought him a wide readership. The novels on which his reputation is based were all published in monthly instalments: *Vanity Fair* (1847–8), *Pendennis*

(1848), *The History of Henry Esmond* (1852), *The Newcomes* (1853–5), and *The Virginians* (1857–9). Thackeray retired from *Punch* in 1854 and became editor of the *Cornhill Magazine* in 1860.

THORNYCROFT, Sir William Hamo (1850–1925)

2a Melbury Road, W14

Sculptor, born in London, the son of Thomas Thornycroft, also sculptor. He studied under his father, at the Royal Academy, and in Italy. He executed many public monuments, including the statues of General Gordon in Trafalgar Square; Oliver Cromwell at Westminster; William Gladstone in the Strand; and the bas-relief of Richard Norman Shaw at New Scotland Yard. He was knighted in 1917 and died in Oxford.

THURLOE, John (1616–68)

Wall of Lincoln's Inn, Chancery Lane WC2

Parliamentarian politician, born at Abbot's Roding, Essex. He studied law and in 1652 was appointed secretary to the Council of State and was a member of Cromwell's second council (1657). After the Restoration he was arrested for high treason but was released one month later.

TOMPION, Thomas (1638–1713), and GRAHAM, George (1673–1751)

69 Fleet Street, EC4

Clockmakers, lived in a house on this site. Both are buried in Westminster Abbey.

TOWNLEY, Charles (1737–1805)

14 Queen Anne's Gate, SW1

Antiquary and collector, lived here.

TREVITHICK, Richard (1771–1833)

University College, Gower Street, WC1

Engineer and inventor, born near Illogan, Cornwall. At the age of nineteen he was an engineer at various Cornish mines. He invented high pressure steam engines and constructed locomotives ten years before Stephenson's earliest one. He introduced his Cornish boiler in 1812 and four years later sailed to Peru to install his engines at the Cerro de Pasco silver mines. He returned to England penniless, in 1827.

Trevithick died at Hartford, Kent. At the centenary of his death it was commemorated by an exhibition of his work at the Science Museum of London.

TURNER, Joseph Mallord William (1775–1851)

119 Cheyne Walk, SW3

Painter, born at 26 Maiden Lane, London, the son of a barber. He entered the Royal Academy School in 1789. Three years later he was elected an associate, and in 1802 he became an academician, at the age of twenty seven. As he never married,

had no expensive habits, and devoted his time entirely to his art, he was able to amass a huge fortune. A great number of his pictures are at the Tate Gallery, including *The Shipwreck*, *Hannibal Crossing the Alps*, etc. He died in London and was buried in St Paul's Cathedral.

23 Queen Anne Street, W1

Turner lived here.

TWAIN, Mark (pseudonym of Samuel Langhorne Clemens, 1833–1910)

23 Tedworth Square, SW3

American writer, born at Florida, Mo. He was apprenticed to a printer in 1848, then worked for his elder brother, a newspaper publisher. He was licensed as a Mississippi river pilot in 1858. At the outbreak of the Civil War, and after a few, inglorious weeks in the Confederate Militia, he went to Nevada. His first book *The Celebrated Jumping Frog of Calaveras Country* was published in 1867. He married Olivia Lengdon in 1870. Mark Twain became the most famous humorist in the United States. His best-known books are *The Adventures of Tom Sawyer*, published in 1876, and his masterpiece *The Adventures of Huckleberry Finn* (1884).

U

UNWIN, Sir Stanley (1884–1968)

13 Handen Road, Heather Green, SE12

Publisher, born here.

V

VANBRUGH, Sir John (1664–1726)

Vanbrugh Castle, Maze Hill, SE10

Architect and dramatist, born in London, the son of a sugar baker of Flemish descent. Educated at King's School, Chester. At the age of nineteen he was sent to France to study, returning to England two years later to take up a commission in the Earl of Huntingdon's Regiment. His play *The Provok'd Wife* was a success in 1697. Afterwards, Vanbrugh turned his attention to architecture. He was appointed architect to the Earl of Carlisle and completed Castle Howard for him in 1714. He was also commissioned to build Blenheim Palace, a gift of the nation to the Duke of Marlborough, and built the Haymarket Opera House. He married Henrietta Maria Yarborough in 1719 and was knighted in 1723.

VAN BUREN, Martin (1782–1862)

7 Stratford Place, W1

American president, born in Albany, N.Y. He was admitted to the bar in 1803 and married Hannah Hoes in 1807. He came to London, as US Ambassador to St James's Court, in 1831. During Andrew Jackson's presidential campaign, van Buren was his adviser. After winning the Presidency, Jackson appointed him Secretary of State, and afterwards Vice President. He eventually succeeded

him, becoming the eighth President of the United States.

VANE, Sir Henry (1612–62)

Gatepost of Vane House, Rosslyn Hill, NW3

English statesman, born at Hadlow, Kent. Educated at Westminster and Magdalen Hall, Oxford. A Puritan, he emigrated to Massachusetts in 1635 to enjoy the free exercise of his religion. He was elected governor in 1636 but a year later he returned to England. In 1640 he was knighted and afterwards elected for Hull in the Short and Long Parliaments. He furnished the supplies for Cromwell's expedition to Scotland. At the Restoration, Vale was imprisoned in the Tower. Although he took no part in Charles I's trial and execution and Charles II granted him a royal pardon, the new Parliament, considering him 'too dangerous to live', demanded his trial on the capital charge. Vane was found guilty and executed on Tower Hill.

VAN GOGH, Vincent Willem (1853–90)

87 Hackford Road, SW9

Painter, born at Groot-Zundert (Brabant), the eldest son of a Protestant pastor. At the age of sixteen he was apprenticed to Goupil & Co., art dealers, first in The Hague, and then in London. Vincent was always desperately poor, being sustained by his younger brother, Theo. In Paris, he met Paul Gauguin and discovered Impressionism. In 1888 he left Paris for Arles, where he was to paint his best pictures. During his last two years, van Gogh suffered a series of mental crises which ended with his attempted suicide and his death two days later.

VOLTAIRE (Francois Marie Arouet de, 1694–1778)

10 Maiden Lane, WC2

French author, born in Paris, the son of a notary. Educated at the College

Louis Le Grand, run by the Jesuits. Voltaire was the dominant figure of the 18th-century European enlightenment. Exiled to England in 1726 and became acquainted with the Duchess of Marlborough and the poet Alexander Pope (see p. 120). He was permitted to return to France in 1729. His best known work is the satirical masterpiece *Candide* (1759).

W

WAKEFIELD, Edward Gibbon (1796–1862)

1–5 Adam Street, WC2

Colonial statesman, born in London, attended Westminster School. At the age of 20 he eloped with Eliza Susan Pattle. After her death, he abducted Ellen Turner, a young heiress, for which Wakefield was sentenced to three years imprisonment in Newgate. There he developed an interest in colonial matters and wrote his famous *Letter from Sydney* (1829). His ideas became the motive force behind the South Australian Company and, as secretary to Lord Durham, influenced the New Zealand Association and the subsequent annexation of New Zealand. He afterwards established the Canterbury Settlement in New Zealand, as a Church of England colony. He spent the last eight years of

his life in retirement, and died in Wellington.

WALLACE, Edgar (1875–1932)

Junction of Fleet Street and Ludgate Circus, EC4

English writer, born in London, the illegitimate son of an actress. He joined the army and served in South Africa. On his return to England he worked for *The Daily Mail*. He was a racehorse breeder, journalist and late editor. His first novel, *The Four Just Men*, was published in 1905, *Sanders of the River* in 1911. He was a prolific author turning out over 170 novels and plays, including *The Clue of the Twisted Candle* and *The Ringer.* Edgar Wallace died suddenly in Hollywood when he was working on the filming of *King Kong.*

6 Tressiliant Crescent, SE4

Edgar Wallace lived here.

WALLACE, Sir William (c. 1274–1305)

St Bartholomew's Hospital, EC1

Scottish patriot. He rebelled against Edward I of England and was defeated at Falkirk. He then travelled to France but eventually returned to Scotland, where a price was set upon his head. He was taken at Robroyston, near Glasgow, by Sir John Menteith —

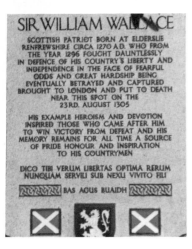

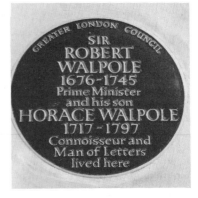

allegedly through treachery — and carried to the Castle of Dumbarton, whence he was sent to London, tried as a traitor, found guilty, hanged, and quartered, the quarters being sent to Newcastle, Berwick, Sterling, and Perth.

WALPOLE, Sir Robert, 1st Earl of Orford (1676–1745)

5 Arlington Street, SW1

Statesman, born at Houghton, Norfolk. Educated at Eton and King's College, Cambridge. Entered Parliament, first for Castle Rising in 1701, and then for King's Lynn, retaining his seat until he was raised to the peerage. In 1708 he was made secretary-at-war and treasurer of the navy in 1710. In 1712, when the Tories took power, he was accused of corruption and sent for a short time to the Tower. After the Whigs regained power Walpole became First Minister from 1721 to 1742. He died in Arlington Street on 18 March 1745.

WALPOLE, Horace, 4th Earl of Orford (1717–97)

Politician and author, youngest son of Sir Robert Walpole. Educated at Eton and King's College, Cambridge. Met the poet Thomas Grey at Eton and later went on the Grand Tour with him. Entered Parliament for Callington in Cornwall in 1741, later exchanging this seat for the family borough of Castle Rising in 1754 and then in 1757 vacating this for the other family seat of King's Lynn. In 1747 purchased the house near Twickenham which was transformed into the Gothic folly known as Strawberry Hill. Established his own printing press and printed Gray's two Pindaric Odes in 1758, as well as his own works. His famous Gothic novel *The Castle of Otranto* was published in 1764 and *The Mysterious Mother* in 1768. Walpole is best known for his gifts as a letter writer, which paint a detailed picture of Walpole's life and interests during the years 1732 to 1797.

WALTER, John (1739–1812)

Gilmore House, 113 Clapham Common, North Side, SW4

Printer and newspaper publisher, born in London, the son of a prosperous coal merchant. After his father's death he inherited his business and played a leading part in

the establishment of a Coal Exchange in London. But then he became a member of Lloyd's, speculated heavily, and failed. In 1784 he acquired an old printing office in Blackfriars, and set up his 'Logographic Office' there. In 1785 he started a small newspaper called *The Daily Universal Register*, renamed *The Times* in 1788.

WARLOCK, Peter (Philip Arnold Heseltine, 1894–1930)

30 Tite Street, SW3

English composer and musicologist, lived here.

WAUGH, Benjamin (1839–1908)

26 Cromms Hill, Greenwich, SE10

Philanthropist and reformer, born at Settle, Yorkshire. After spending several years in business he entered the Congregational ministry in 1865,

devoting himself to children. He served on the London School Board from 1870 to 1877 and was one of the founders of the London Society for the Prevention of Cruelty to Children. He edited *The Sunday Magazine* from 1874 to 1896 and died at Westcliff, Essex.

WEBER, Carl Maria Friedrich Ernst von (1786–1826)

103 Great Portland Street, W1

German composer and pianist, born in Eutin, near Lübeck, Germany.

Became the pupil of Abt Vogler in Vienna in 1803 and through Vogler's influence became conductor of the Breslau Opera. Married Carolina Brandt, the singer, in 1817 and the following year composed the famous *Mass in G. Der Freischütz* was completed in 1820 and his masterpiece, *Oberon*, written for Charles Kemnie of the Covent Garden Theatre, first performed in London in March 1826. He died on 4 June that year and was buried in St Mary's, Moorfields. In 1844 his remains were transferred to Dresden.

WEIZMANN, Chaim (1874–1952)

67 Addison Road, W14

Jewish scientist and statesman, born in Motol, Russian Poland. Educated in Germany and Switzerland. After being a lecturer in biochemistry in Geneva, he held the same post in Manchester. During the First World War he worked for the Admiralty and

discovered the use of acetone in naval explosives. Instrumental in bringing about the Balfour Declaration of 1917 and was president of the Zionist Organization. When Israel was created in 1948, he became its first president. He died at Rehovoth, Palestine.

WELLS, Herbert George (1866–1946)

13 Hanover Terrace, NW1

Author, born in Bromley and apprenticed to a draper. After a spell as a teacher he turned to journalism and writing. Wells's novels divide themselves into three broad groups: fantasy and scientific romances such as *The Time Machine* (1895) and *War of the Worlds* (1898), novels such as *The History of Mr Polly* (1910) which deal with contemporary urban life and the 'little man', and the novels of ideas such as *Tono-Bungay* (1909). He also

wrote short stories (e.g. *The Country of the Blind*, 1911), as well as essays on a wide variety of subjects. His *Outline of History* and *Short History of the World* were published in 1920 and 1922 respectively and his *Science of Life*, written with Julian Huxley and his son G.P. Wells, appeared in 1929. Wells reflected on his life in the fascinating *Experiment in Autobiography* (1934). He married his cousin Isabel Wells in 1891, but the marriage was a failure and he subsequently married Amy Robbins. He died here in Hanover Terrace in 1946.

WESLEY, Charles (1707–88)

1 Wheatley Street, W1

Evangelist and hymn writer, born at Epworth, Lincolnshire, brother of John Wesley. Educated at Westminster and Christ Church, Oxford. Ordained in 1735. His conversion occurred on Whitsunday

(21 May) 1738.
Evangelized in London 1738–9 and
then settled in Bristol. Wesley wrote
over 6,000 hymns, including 'Love
divine, all loves excelling' and 'Jesu,
lover of my soul'. He married Sarah
Gwynne in 1749 and died in London.

WHISTLER, James Abbott McNeil
(1834–1903)

96 Cheyne Walk, SW3

American artist, provoker of the
famous lawsuit against Ruskin in
which Whistler was awarded a
farthing damages. Lived here.

WHITBREAD, Samuel
(1758–1815)

Chiswell Street, EC1

Politician and founder of the famous
brewing firm which bears his name.
Educated at Eton and Oxford and

then entered Parliament.

WHITTINGTON, Sir Richard
(c. 1358–1423)

20 College Hill, EC4

English merchant. He married Alice,
daughter of Sir Ivo Fitzwaryn, a
Dorset knight and landowner.
Whittington was four times Mayor of
London. He made large loans to both
Henry IV and Henry V. At his death

he bequeathed his vast fortune to charitable and public purposes.

WILBERFORCE, William (1759–1833)

44 Cadogan Place, SW1

Philanthropist and opponent of slavery, born in Hull. Educated at Hull grammar school and St John's College, Cambridge. Entered Parliament for Hull in 1780 and for Yorkshire in 1784. He remained loyal to Pitt throughout his life. Helped to found the Abolition Society, designed to end the slave trade, in 1787. After his marriage in 1797 and the acquisition of a house at Clapham, Wilberforce and his evangelical friends, previously called 'The Saints', became known as 'The Clapham Sect'. Wilberforce was a co-founder of the *Christian Observer* (1801) and author of *A Practical View of Christianity* (1797). He died at his cousin's house in Cadogan Place and is buried in Westminster Abbey.

Broomwood Road, SW11

Wilberforce lived here.

WILDE, Oscar Fingall O'Flahertie Wills (1854–1900)

34 Tite Street, SW3

Poet, dramatist, and wit, educated at Trinity College, Dublin, and Magdalen College, Oxford. At Oxford he won the Newdigate Prize for his poem *Ravenna* and cultivated the aesthetic style caricatured by Gilbert and Sullivan in *Patience*. His first volume of *Poems* appeared in 1881 and his novel *The Picture of Dorian Gray* in 1891. Then came a string of sparkling comedies: *Lady Windermere's Fan* (1892), *A Woman of No Importance* (1893, *An Ideal Husband* (1894), and *The Importance of Being Earnest* (1895). The play *Salomé*, written in French,

was published in 1893 and performed in Paris in 1896. He brought an unsuccessful action for libel against the Marquis of Queensberry, father of his friend Lord Alfred Douglas, in 1895. The homosexual practices uncovered by the trial resulted in Wilde's being sentenced to two years' hard labour, the experience of which gave rise to *The Ballad of Reading Gaol* (1898) and *De Profundis* (1905). After his release Wilde lived at Berneval and later in Paris, where he died.

WILHELMINA, Helena Pauline Maria of Orange-Nassau, Queen of the Netherlands (1880–1962)

77 Chester Square, SW1

Born in The Hague, daughter of King Wilhelm III. She succeeded to the throne in 1890. Married to Henry, Duke of Mecklenburg-Schwerin, in 1901. Her only child, Princess Juliana, was born in 1909.

Wilhelmina abdicated in 1948, being succeeded by Juliana. She died at her Palace in Het Loo.

WILLAN, Dr Robert (1757–1812)

10 Bloomsbury Square, WC1

English dermatologist who became famous for his descriptions of the lesion known as *lupus vulgaris* and for being the first English physician to classify skin diseases. He is the author of *The Description and Treatment of Cutaneous Diseases* (1798–1808). He died at Madeira.

WILLOUGHBY, Sir Hugh (*d.* 1554)

King Edward Memorial Park, Shadwell, E1

English explorer. In 1553 he set out with three ships, the *Bona Esperanza* (his own ship), the *Bona Confidenza*, and the *Edward Bonaventura* to search for a north-east passage to Cathay. The ship commanded by Richard Chancellor

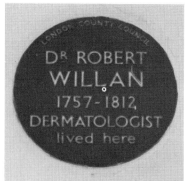

THIS TABLET IS IN MEMORY OF
SIR HUGH WILLOUGHBY, STEPHEN BOROUGH,
WILLIAM BOROUGH, SIR MARTIN FROBISHER
AND OTHER NAVIGATORS WHO, IN THE LATTER
HALF OF THE SIXTEENTH CENTURY, SET SAIL
FROM THIS REACH OF THE RIVER THAMES NEAR
RATCLIFF CROSS
TO EXPLORE THE NORTHERN SEAS.

ERECTED BY THE LONDON COUNTY COUNCIL, 1922

parted company with the other two in a storm and Willoughby and his companion vessel eventually reached Russian Lapland, where they decided to winter. Here Willoughby and his sixty-two companions died of cold and scurvy. Their bodies were found a year later by Russian sailors.

WILSON, Edward Adrian (1872–1912)

Vicarage Crescent, SW11

British naturalist and Antarctic explorer, lived here.

WINANT, John Gilbert (1889–1947)

7 Aldorf Street, W1

American diplomat, educated at Princeton. He saw service with the USAF during the First World War. Succeeded Joseph Kennedy as

men with the aim of recapturing Quebec and expelling the French from Canada. The expedition landed below Quebec in June 1759 and initially the French, under Montcalm, seemed in an unassailable position. But at dawn on 13 September Wolfe and a contingent of some 3,000 men scaled the Heights of Abraham and took the French by surprise. Montcalm was killed in the battle that ensued and Wolfe was mortally wounded by a musket ball. His last words were 'Now, God be praised, I will die in peace.'

ambassador to London, and was in London during the German bombings. He took his own life in 1947.

WINGFIELD, Major Walter Clopton (1833–1912)

33 St George's Square, SW1

Father of lawn tennis, lived here.

WOLFE, James (1727–59)

McCarthey House, Greenwich Park, SE10

Soldier, born at Westerham, Kent, eldest son of General Edward Wolfe. In 1741 he received a commission in the marines but later transferred to the 12th Foot. Saw action at the Battle of Dettingen. After commanding a brigade under General Amherst in the expedition against Cape Breton, Wolfe was given command by Pitt of a force of 9,000

WOOD, Sir Henry Joseph (1869–1944)

4 Elsworthy Road, NW3

English musician and conductor, born in London. Attended the Royal Academy of Music. Engaged by Robert Newman in 1895 to conduct a series of Promenade Concerts at the

biography of Elizabeth Browning's dog, *Flush* (1933). Leonard Woolf's works include *The Village and the Jungle* (1913) and *After the Deluge* (1931, 1939) and he was a member of the Fabian Society from 1916. He and Virginia were at the centre of what became known as the Bloomsbury Group of writers and artists (see p. 171). Suffering from depression during the middle years of the Second World War, Virginia drowned herself in Sussex.

29 Fitzroy Square, W1

Virginia Woolf lived here from 1907 to 1911.

Queen's Hall which became an annual event. After the Queen's Hall was destroyed during the Second World War the concerts moved to the Albert Hall. Wood was knighted in 1911.

WOOLF, Leonard Sidney (1800–1969), and Virginia (1882–1941)

Hogarth House, Paradise Road, Richmond

Virginia Woolf, daughter of Sir Leslie Stephen, married Leonard Woolf in 1912 and five years later they founded the Hogarth Press together. Virginia's first novel, *The Voyage Out*, was published in 1915 and followed by over half a dozen others, including *Jacob's Room* (1922), *Mrs Dalloway* (1925), and *To the Lighthouse* (1927). She also wrote essays (collected in *The Common Reader*, 1925 and 1932, and *A Room of One's Own*, 1929) and a charming

WOOLNER, Thomas (1826–92)

29 Welbeck Street, W1

Poet and sculpter, born at Hadleigh, Suffolk. Attended the Royal Academy

School. After he met D.G. Rossetti (p. 128) and Leigh Hunt (p. 74) he became a member of the Pre-Raphaelite Brotherhood. His poems were published in *Germ*, the Brotherhood's magazine. After a period in Australia 1852–4 he returned to London and sculpted many famous contemporaries, including Tennyson and John Stuart Mill (p. 100). Professor of Sculpture at the Royal Academy 1877–9.

WREN, Sir Christopher (1632–1723)

Cardinal's Wharf, 49 Bankside, SE1

Architect, born at East Knoyle, Wiltshire, the son of a clergyman. Educated at Westminster School and Wadham College, Oxford. Elected to a fellowship at All Souls in 1653. Professor of astronomy at Gresham College, London, 1657; Savilian professor of astronomy at Oxford 1661. Wren was one of the founders of the Royal Society. The first building erected from a design by Wren was the chapel of Pembroke College, Cambridge (1663). Over the next three years he designed the Sheldonian Theatre at Oxford and the library at Trinity College, Cambridge. The Great Fire of London in 1666 was seen by Wren as an opportunity for rebuilding the city on a grand scale, but his plans were not implemented. He was however selected as the architect for the new St Paul's Cathedral (1675–1710) and for the many other churches destroyed in the fire. Other notable Wren buildings included the Greenwich Observatory, the Ashmolean Museum at Oxford, the Chelsea Hospital, and Marlborough House. He was knighted in 1672 and became president of the Royal Society in 1680. He was buried in his masterpiece, St Paul's.

See also Catherine of Aragon (p. 28).

Y

**YEATS, William Butler
(1865–1939)**

5 Woburn Walk, WC1

Irish poet and dramatist, born in
Dublin, the son of the painter John
Butler Yeats and brother of Jack Yeats,
also a painter. Educated at the
Godolphin School, Hammersmith, and
the Dublin High School. Studied art in
Dublin for three years before turning to
literature in his early twenties. His
deep commitment to Irish nationalism
and to the cultural and literary
heritage of Ireland, as well as a
penchant for the mystical and the
occult, underpin all his work. With
Lady Gregory he helped found the Irish
National Theatre and from 1922 to
1928 he was a sentator of the Irish Free
State. His early passion for Irish
folklore and legends showed itself in
*Fairy and Folk Tales of the Irish
Peasantry* (1888), *The Wanderings of
Oisin* (1889), and *The Celtic Twilight*
(1893), whilst with these themes was
intertwined his unrequited love for the
beautiful Maud Gonne. He moved away
from the pre-Raphaelite, 1890s style in
such collections as *In the Seven Woods*
(1903) and *Responsibilities* (1914).
Later collections include *Michael
Robartes and the Dancer* (1921), *The
Winding Stair* (1929), *A Full Moon in*

WILLIAM BUTLER YEATS
IRISH POET AND DRAMATIST
LIVED IN THIS HOUSE
THEN KNOWN AS 18 WOBURN BUILDINGS
FROM 1895 TO 1919

March (1935) and the complex commentary on the symbolism of his poetry, *A Vision* (1925). He received the Nobel Prize for Literature in 1923 and died in the South of France. He is buried at Drumcliff in Co. Sligo.

23 Fitzroy Road, NW1

Yeats lived here from 1867 to 1873.

YOUNG, Thomas (1773–1829)

48 Welbeck Street, W1

Physicist and Egyptologist, born at Milverton, Somerset. Educated at London, Edinburgh, Göttingen, and Cambridge. From 1801 to 1803 he was professor of natural philosophy at the Royal Institution. His researches helped to establish the wave theory of light, and in 1801 he discovered the principle of interference of light and described astigmatism. He also was one of the first to work on the deciphering of Egyptian hieroglyphic inscriptions. He died in London in 1829.

Z

ZOFFANY, Johann (1733–1810)
65 Strand-on-the-Green, W4

Painter, born at Frankfurt-am-Mein. Educated in Italy. He came to England in 1761 and exhibited at the Society of Artists from 1762 to 1769 and at the Royal Academy (of which he became a founder-member) from 1770 to 1800. Received the patronage of George III and became a fashionable painter of portraits and conversation pieces. His *Hunter Delivering a Lecture on Anatomy Before the Members of the Royal Academy* is at the Royal College of

Physicians. He died here in Strand-on-the-Green, Middlesex.

Part 2

SELECTED HISTORICAL SITES

ALDERSGATE

1 Aldersgate Street, EC1

Called originally Ealdredsgate. From this gate John Day, the leading printer of Elizabeth I's reign, issued his editions of Foxe's *Book of Martyrs* and Roger Ascham's *The Schoolmaster*. The gate was severely damaged during the Great Fire of 1666 but subsequently repaired. It was demolished in 1761.

ALDGATE

88 Aldgate Street, EC3

The main east gate of the ancient city of London. The dwelling over the gate was once occupied by Chaucer. The insurrection led by Wat Tyler in 1381 entered the city through this gate, which was demolished in 1760.

ANTI-CORN-LAW OFFICES

1 Whitefriars Street, EC4

The Corn Laws, restricting the importation of foreign corn, were first introduced in 1815 and were the

subject of intense debate and controversy in the first half of the 19th century. The focus of opposition to the laws was the Anti-Corn-Law league, founded in 1839 and led by Richard Cobden (1804–65) and John Bright (1811–89). As a result of agitations by the League and the Irish famine of 1845 the Corn Law was repealed in 1846.

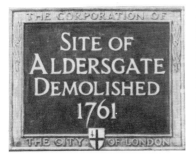

St Bartholomew's Hospital

West Smithfield, EC1

Whilst on a pilgrimage to Rome, Rahere (supposedly jester to Henry I before entering the priesthood) vowed to build a church and hospital in honour of St Bartholomew. The work was begun in 1123 on land granted to Rahere (*d*. 1144) by King Henry. Rahere is also the supposed founder of St Bartholomew's Church, Smithfield. William Harvey, discoverer of the circulation of the blood, was a physician at Bart's 1609–43.

Barton Street

Barton Street, W1

Derives its name from Barton Booth who owned several properties in Westminster. His wife was the mistress of the Duke of Marlborough.

Bell Inn

Bell Inn Yard, EC3

Situated in Bell Inn Yard, from where Richard Queyney addressed a letter to William Shakespeare, the only one known to exist.

(SECOND) BETHLEHEM HOSPITAL

9 London Wall, EC2

The Hospital of St Mary of Bethlehem (corrupted to Bedlam) was founded in 1247 as a priory but by 1402 it was being used as a hospital for lunatics. It was granted to the mayor and citizens of London at the Dissolution and in 1547 was incorporated as a royal foundation for the reception of lunatics. A new hospital was built in Moorfields in 1676, replaced by another building in the Lambeth Road in 1815.

BLACKHEATH HALL

Blackheath, SE10

Film studio of the CPO and the Crown Film Units 1933–42.

BLACKWELL HALL

Guildhall Yard, EC2

Derives its name from Thomas Bakewell. Established during the reign of Richard II by the Mayor and the Corporation of the City as the sole market for the wool trade. Destroyed by the Great Fire but rebuilt in 1672.

BLOOMSBURY GROUP

Bloomsbury Square, WC1

Members included Virginia Woolf, E.M. Forster, Clive Bell, Roger Fry, and Lytton Strachey, author of *Eminent Victorians* (1918) and a biography of Queen Victoria (1921). The area was

first known as Blemond, named after the Earl of Blemond, a vassal of William I, and was developed during the 18th century by the dukes of Bedford.

19–20 Bow Street, WC2

Former residents include the novelist Henry Fielding (1707–54), author of *Tom Jones* (1749); the woodcarver Grinling Gibbons (1648–1721); and the Restoration dramatist William Wycherley (*c.* 1640–1716), author of *The Country Wife* (1675).

BULL INN

Bishopgate Street, EC2

A hostelry for travellers and coach office, also used for the performance of plays. It was pulled down in 1866.

CAMPDEN HILL SQUARE

Campden Hill Square, W11

Laid out in 1826 by Joshua Flesher Hanson.

CATO STREET CONSPIRACY

1a Cato Street, W1

A group of conspirators met in Cato Street in 1820 to plan the assassination of all the cabinet ministers, while they attended a dinner hosted by the Duke of Wellington, in revenge for the so-called Massacre of Peterloo (an ironical reference to the Battle of Waterloo), where eleven people — among them two women — were killed and about four hundred were wounded during an

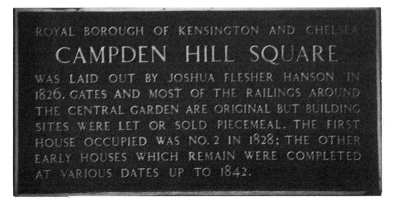

ROYAL BOROUGH OF KENSINGTON AND CHELSEA

CAMPDEN HILL SQUARE

WAS LAID OUT BY JOSHUA FLESHER HANSON IN 1826. GATES AND MOST OF THE RAILINGS AROUND THE CENTRAL GARDEN ARE ORIGINAL BUT BUILDING SITES WERE LET OR SOLD PIECEMEAL. THE FIRST HOUSE OCCUPIED WAS NO. 2 IN 1828; THE OTHER EARLY HOUSES WHICH REMAIN WERE COMPLETED AT VARIOUS DATES UP TO 1842.

anti-government meeting in St Peter's Fields, Manchester. Betrayed by one of their members the conspirators were arrested; five were hanged and the rest exiled to Australia.

CHELSEA CHINA

15 Lawrence Street, SW3

Established at Chelsea around 1730 under the direction of German porcelain makers and much favoured by George II. Chelsea China was manufactured in a house at the north end of Lawrence Street from 1745 to 1784, when the factory was relocated to Derby. This site was also the home

ROYAL BOROUGH OF KENSINGTON AND CHELSEA

THE CHELSEA
PHYSIC GARDEN

WAS ESTABLISHED BY THE WORSHIPFUL SOCIETY OF APOTHECARIES OF LONDON IN 1673 AND IS THE OLDEST BOTANIC GARDEN, AFTER OXFORD, IN ENGLAND. A STATUE OF SIR HANS SLOANE, AN EARLY BENEFACTOR, SCULPTED BY MICHAEL RYSBRACH, STANDS IN THE CENTRE. IN 1899 RESPONSIBILITY FOR THE GARDEN PASSED TO THE TRUSTEES OF THE LONDON PAROCHIAL CHARITIES.

of the novelist Tobias Smollett (1721–71), author of *Roderick Random* (1748) and *Peregrine Pickle* (1751).

CHELSEA PHYSIC GARDEN

Established by the Worshipful Society of Apothecaries in 1673.

CHESHIRE CHEESE

Wine Court, 142 Fleet Street, EC4

A famous tavern opened in 1667 and frequented by journalists and writers, including Dr Johnson (see p. 79).

CHISWICK SQUARE

W4

Immortalized by Thackeray (see p. 143) in *Vanity Fair* (1847–8). The houses each side were built about 1680, Boston House, built in 1740 on the site of a previous mansion, lies on the picturesque old square behind large iron gates.

CHRIST'S HOSPITAL

Newgate Street, EC1

Also known as the Bluecoat School. Founded under a royal charter of Edward VI in 1552 as a school for poor children, the buildings were severely damaged during the Great Fire. Pupils included Coleridge, Charles Lamb, and Leigh Hunt. The school is now situated in Horsham.

CITY OF LONDON SCHOOL

3 Milk Street, EC2

Designed by J.B. Bunning, the city architect. The first stone was laid by Lord Brougham (1835). Subsequently removed to the Thames Embankment.

CLAPHAM SECT, Holy Trinity Church

Clapham Common, SW4

Attended by William Wilberforce (see p. 157) and other members of the Clapham Sect.

CLINK PRISON

Clink Street, SE1

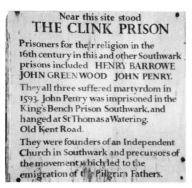

Originally called the Liberty of the Clink, an area surrounding the palace of the bishops of Winchester in Southwark, it subsequently became a prison (hence the slang term 'in clink'). It was closed down in 1842.

COLLINS' MUSIC-HALL

10–11 Islington Green, N1

Founded by the Irish comedian Sam Collins. A number of famous performers played here, including Charlie Chaplin and Harry Lauder.

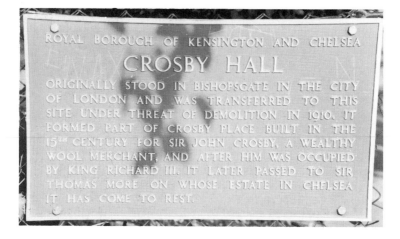

COMPTER, GILTSPUR STREET

2 Giltspur Street, EC1

A short street leading to Smithfield where knights rode to the tournaments.

CROSBY HALL

Cheyne Walk, SW3

Build by Sir John Crosby in 1466 and erected on the site of a Roman villa in land belonging to the Priory of St Helen. Sir Thomas More lived here.

DAVIES AMPHITHEATRE

4 Bear Garden Street, E1

The last bear-baiting ring of Bankside.

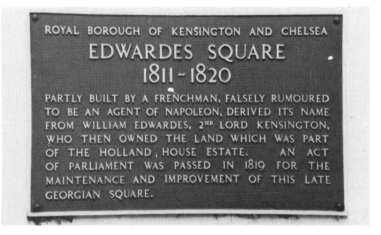

ROYAL BOROUGH OF KENSINGTON AND CHELSEA
EDWARDES SQUARE
1811 - 1820

PARTLY BUILT BY A FRENCHMAN, FALSELY RUMOURED TO BE AN AGENT OF NAPOLEON, DERIVED ITS NAME FROM WILLIAM EDWARDES, 2ND LORD KENSINGTON, WHO THEN OWNED THE LAND WHICH WAS PART OF THE HOLLAND HOUSE ESTATE. AN ACT OF PARLIAMENT WAS PASSED IN 1819 FOR THE MAINTENANCE AND IMPROVEMENT OF THIS LATE GEORGIAN SQUARE.

DEVIL TAVERN

1 Fleet Street, EC4

Originally called St Dunstan's Tavern, it became known as the Devil Tavern because of its sign showing St Dunstan pulling the devil by the nose.

EDWARDES SQUARE

Earls Terrace, W8

Derives its name from William Edwardes, 2nd Lord Kensington. Built by a Frenchman during the Napoleonic wars.

THE CORPORATION OF
SITE OF
THE DEVIL
TAVERN
DEMOLISHED 1787.
THE CITY OF LONDON

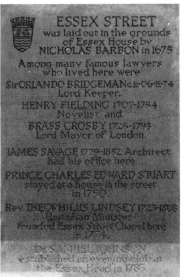

ESSEX STREET was laid out in the grounds of Essex House by NICHOLAS BARBON in 1675

Among many famous lawyers who lived here were

Sir ORLANDO BRIDGEMAN c.1606-1674 Lord Keeper,

HENRY FIELDING 1707-1784 Novelist and

BRASS CROSBY 1725-1793 Lord Mayor of London.

JAMES SAVAGE 1779-1852 Architect had his office here.

PRINCE CHARLES EDWARD STUART stayed at a house in the street in 1750.

Rev. THEOPHILUS LINDSEY 1723-1808 Unitarian Minister Founded Essex Street Chapel here in 1774.

Dr SAMUEL JOHNSON established an evening club at the Essex Head in 1783.

THE SITE OF
17 OSNABURGH STREET
WHERE
THE
FABIAN SOCIETY
WAS FOUNDED
IN 1884

ESSEX STREET

Essex Street, WC2

Derives its name from Robert Devereaux, Earl of Essex, Queen Elizabeth's favourite who was executed for plotting against her.

FABIAN SOCIETY

The White House, Osnaburgh Street, NW1

Founded in 1884. Members included Beatrice and Sidney Webb, George Bernard Shaw (see p. 134), E. Nesbit and Annie Besant. Its main objective was social improvement through evolutionary socialism rather than violent revolution.

FRENCH PROTESTANT CHURCH

2 Aldersgate Street, EC1

Built by Edward VI for French Protestant refugees. Demolished in 1888.

FURNIVAL'S INN

Prudential Insurance Building, High Holborn, EC2

An Inn of Court, formerly attached to Lincoln's Inn, named after Sir William Furnival. Charles Dickens wrote *The Pickwick Papers* here.

GLOBE THEATRE

Park Street, SE1

Erected by the Burbages (James and Richard) in Southwark in 1599 using materials from the Old Theatre on the north side of the river. It was a circular wooden building partly

SITE OF THE
FRENCH PROTESTANT
CHURCH
DEMOLISHED
1888

SITE OF
FURNIVAL'S
INN
DEMOLISHED
1897

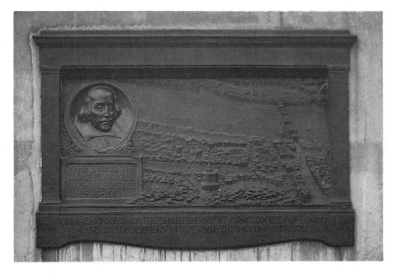

thatched and on 29 June 1613, during a performance of a play called *All Is True*, the thatch caught fire and the building was destroyed. It was rebuilt in 1614. Shakespeare, who also acted there, had a share in the theatre, which was pulled down in 1664. There are now plans to build a replica of the Elizabethan building on the site.

GREYFRIARS MONASTERY

106 Newgate Street, EC1

This order of monks arrived at England during the reign of Henry III (1224) and were dissolved by Henry VIII.

HENRY VIII'S MANOR HOUSE

Cheyne Walk, SW3

Demolished in 1753. Its last occupant was Sir Hans Sloane (see p. 136).

HIPPODROME RACE COURSE

St John's Church, Ladbroke Grove, W11

On the site now occupied by St John's Church (1845) was the Hippodrome Race Course, opened in June 1837. It closed down in 1841 because of competition from Ascot and Epsom.

JOHN BRAY'S HOUSE

13 Little Britain, EC1

The scene of Charles Wesley's conversion, 21 May 1738. For Wesley see p. 155.

JOINERS AND CEILERS COMPANY

Upper Thames Street, EC4

First incorporated by letters patent during the reign of Queen Elizabeth I under the name of The Master and Wardens of the Faculty of Joiners and Ceilers of London.

KENNINGTON PALACE

Kennington Road, SE1

Built by the Black Prince c.1350.

Demolished in 1531. Now Edinburgh House.

Ramsay MacDonald in 1924 and 1929–31.

LABOUR PARTY HOUSE

Caroon House, Farringdon Street, EC4

The Labour Party was founded in 1900 by the trade unions and the Independent Labour party. It became the main opposition party in 1922 and formed a minority government under

LINDSEY HOUSE

100 Cheyne Walk, SW3

Built in 1674 incorporating a house built on the site of Sir Thomas More's farm. The house was sold in 1751 to the Moravian Brethren and was later occupied by the eminent engineers Brunel, father and son.

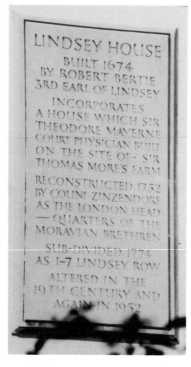

house here in Lombard Street early in the 18th century that became the origin of the association of merchants, shipowners, and underwriters that still bears his name.

LONDON HOUSE

171 Aldersgate Street, EC1

The residence of the bishop of London after the Restoration. Here Princess Anne slept on her flight to Nottingham after the landing of William, Prince of Orange in 1688.

LLOYD'S COFFEE HOUSE

15 Lombard Street, EC3

Edward Lloyd (*d. c.*1730) kept a coffee

LORDS CRICKET GROUND

Dorset Square, NW1

Thomas Lord (1755–1832) established a cricket ground in Dorset Square in 1787. In 1814 the ground was moved to its present site.

LORINERS' HALL

London Wall, EC2

Loriners (or Lorimers) were originally bit-makers or spurriers. They were first incorporated as a livery company during the reign of Queen Anne.

MAY FAIR

Trebeck Street, W1

Site of the ancient fair after which the district was named.

MITRE TAVERN

37 Fleet Street, EC4

A favourite haunt of poets and dramatists in the age of Shakespeare and Ben Jonson. Not to be confused with the Mitre Tavern in Mitre Court frequented by Dr Johnson, Boswell, and Goldsmith.

MOOR GATE

Moorgate, EC2

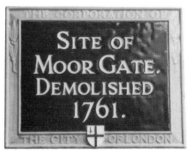

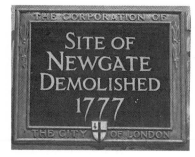

A gate in the old walls of the City of London, built in 1515 and opening on to the moor or 'great fen' to the north, drained in 1527. It was demolished in 1761.

NEWGATE

Newgate Street, EC1

The main west gate of the ancient city of London, where Watling Street reached the city. Its gate-house was a

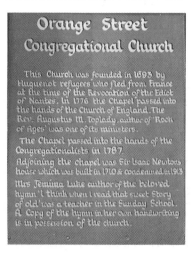

prison from about the 12th century and was enlarged and rebuilt from funds left by Sir Richard Whittington (see p. 156). It was burned down in 1780 in the Gordon Riots, rebuilt, and demolished again in 1902, the site being used to build the Central Criminal Court. The gate itself was demolished in 1777.

NORTHUMBERLAND HOUSE

2 Aldersgate Street, EC1

Formerly a residence of the Percy family, including Henry Percy (1364–1403), the famous Hotspur.

ORANGE STREET CONGREGATIONAL CHURCH

Orange Street, WC2

Founded in 1693 by Huguenot refugees.

PARISH CLERKS' COMPANY

Wood Street, EC2

Licensed as a guild in 1233 under the name of the Fraternity of St Nicholas.

Dissolved by Henry VIII. A new Charter was granted by James I (1611).

PASQUA ROSEE'S HEAD

St Michael's Alley, EC3

Pasqua Rosee, a Turk from Smyrna, opened the first coffee house in London here in 1652.

PETERBOROUGH COURT

143 Fleet Street, EC4

Formerly the hostel of the Abbots of Peterborough. Rebuilt after the Great Fire of London. The land remained in the possession of the diocese of Peterborough until acquired by the proprietor of the *Daily Telegraph* in 1863.

POULTERS' HALL

King Edward Street, EC1

Destroyed during the Great Fire of London.

POST HOUSE YARD

Paultenen Hall, St Martin's-le-Grand, EC1

The first postmarks were struck here in the reign of Charles II.

ROSEBANK

The Ridgeway, Mill Hill, NW7

Quaker meeting house.

ROYAL COLLEGE OF PHYSICIANS

Warwick Lane, EC4

The College was established by Thomas Linacre, physician to Henry VIII, incorporated in 1518. After the Great Fire it moved to Warwick Lane and then to Pall Mall East.

ROYAL SOCIETY FOR THE ENCOURAGEMENT OF ARTS MANUFACTURERS AND COMMERCE

8 Adam Street, WC2

Designed by Robert and James Adam. Foundation laid 28 March 1772, completed 24 April 1774.

ST ANDREW HUBBARD

16 Eastcheap, EC3

Destroyed during the Great Fire and was not rebuilt. The parish of St Andrew Hubbard was united to St Mary-at-Hill.

ST AUGUSTINE PAPEY

65 St Mary Axe, EC3

In the 15th century this was united to the parish church of All Hallows in the Wall. Destroyed during the reign of Edward VI, it was replaced by a stable and hayloft and the churchyard was converted into a garden.

ST BARTHOLOMEW THE GREAT

Cloth Fair, EC1

Founded in 1123. The eastern portion of the church is preserved. Rahere, the first prior, is represented in effigy in a canopied tomb on the north side of the altar. Hogarth and his two sisters were baptised here.

ST BENET GRACECHURCH

Gracechurch Street, EC3

Called 'Grasschurch' for the nearby herb market. Destroyed by the Great Fire, was rebuilt by Sir Christopher Wren (1685) and pulled down in 1867. The site and the material were sold to build St Benet's in the Mile End Road.

ST DUNSTAN

St Dunstan Lane, EC3

THE CHURCH OF ST DUNSTAN IN THE EAST STOOD ON THIS SITE FROM ANCIENT TIMES.

SIR CHRISTOPHER WREN REBUILT THE CHURCH AFTER THE GREAT FIRE OF 1666 AND THE ONLY PART OF HIS DESIGN WHICH SURVIVES IS THE TOWER.

THE REMAINDER OF THE CHURCH WAS REBUILT IN 1817 AND DESTROYED BY ENEMY ACTION IN 1941.

THIS GARDEN WAS CREATED BY THE CORPORATION OF LONDON AND OPENED BY THE RT. HON. THE LORD MAYOR SIR PETER STUDD KT. MA. DSC ON 21st JUNE 1971.

Rebuilt on the site of the church destroyed by the Great Fire. The tower and the spire were by Sir Christopher Wren (see p. 162). Destroyed during the Second World War.

ST GABRIEL

Plantation House 3034, Fenchurch Street, EC3

Destroyed in the Great Fire but not

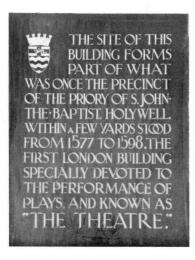

rebuilt. St Margaret Patten became the parish church.

ST JOHN THE BAPTIST (PRIORY OF)

86–8 Curtain Road, EC2

Near here stood the first purpose-built theatre in England, erected by James Burbage (*d.* 1597) and known as The Theatre. Materials from this were used to construct the Globe Theatre in Southwark (see p. 178) in 1598.

ST JOHN THE EVANGELIST

1 Watling Street, Bank of America, EC4

Destroyed in the Great Fire and was not rebuilt. The site is now occupied by the Bank of America.

ST LAWRENCE JEWRY

Gresham Street, EC2

Destroyed in the Great Fire and rebuilt by Sir Christopher Wren. Geoffrey Bollein, a former lord mayor and ancestor of Anne Boleyn, was buried here in 1463.

ST. LAWRENCE. JEWRY.

St. Lawrence Jewry is so called because the original Twelfth Century Church stood on the Eastern side of the City, then occupied by the Jewish Community.

That Church, built in 1136, was destroyed in the Great Fire of London of 1666.

The building which replaced it was designed by Sir Christopher Wren in 1680.

Almost completely destroyed by fire in 1940, this time as the result of action by the King's enemies, it was restored in 1957 in the tradition of Wren's building

St. Lawrence Jewry is now the Church of the Corporation of London.

ST LEONARD EASTCHEAP

Eastcheap, EC3

Also called St Leonard Milk Church after its builder, William Melker. A portion of the old burial ground still remains.

ST LEONARD'S

37 Foster Lane, EC2

Destroyed by the Great Fire and was not rebuilt. Francis Quarles the poet (1592–1644) was buried here.

ST MARTIN

St Martin's-le-Grand, EC1

Site of a collegiate church and sanctuary. Founded in 1056 by the Earl of Essex and his brother. William of Wykeham (founder of Winchester) rebuilt the cloisters of the chapter house. At the dissolution it was demolished.

ST MARTIN OUTWICH

39 Threadneedle Street, EC2

Founded by the Outwich family. Although it escaped the Great Fire it was seriously damaged by the Bishopgate fire of 1765. Samuel Pepys

Cockerell designed a new church, but this was demolished in 1874.

ST MARY COLE

36 Old Jewry, EC2

Thomas à Becket (see p. 131) was baptised here. Destroyed by the Great Fire and not rebuilt.

ST MARY-LE-BOW

Cheapside, EC2

The original church was built during

ST.MARY-LE-BOW CHURCH
The Church of Bow Bells

This Church, built in 1680 by Sir Christopher Wren and restored after war damage in 1964, replaced the 11th century church which was burnt in the Great Fire. The Norman crypt, in which is found the Court of Arches, still survives. The tower and steeple are among Wren's finest achievements and house the famous Bow Bells within whose sound a true cockney is born.

the reign of William the Conqueror but was destroyed during the Great Fire and rebuilt by Sir Christopher Wren. The new bells were installed in 1762 and rung for the first time on George III's birthday that year. It is said that people born within the sound of Bow bells are true Cockneys.

St Mary Woolchurch Haw

Walbrook, WC4

Damaged during the Great Fire, was repaired by Sir Christopher Wren. The new church was designed by his assistant Nicholas Hawksmoor (1716). The church was closed in 1889.

St Michael Bassishaw

Basinghall Street, EC2

Destroyed by the Great Fire and rebuilt by Sir Christopher Wren in 1679. Demolished in 1900.

St Mildred's Church

Poultry (Midland Bank), EC2

Destroyed in the Great Fire and rebuilt by Wren. The poet Shelley (see p. 134) married Mary Godwin here in 1816. Demolished in 1872.

St Paul's School

4 Newgate Street, EC1

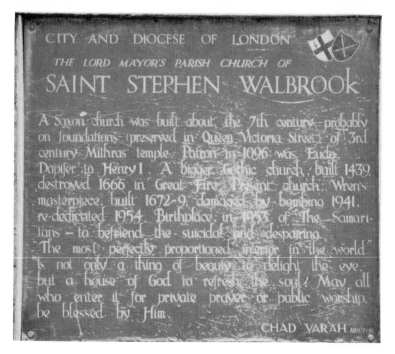

The Dean of St Paul's, Dr John Colet, established the school in 1512. Pupils of the school include the poet John Milton (see p. 102) and the astronomer Edmond Halley (1656–1742).

ST STEPHEN WALBROOK
Walbrook Street, EC4

Destroyed in the Great Fire. Rebuilt by Wren but damaged by bombs during the Second World War.

stood on the site which was given by King Edgar to King Kenneth of Scotland. Known worldwide by its association with the London Metropolitan Police. The site was purchased in 1886 and Richard Norman Shaw commissioned to design and construct the new building. New Scotland Yard became the headquarters of the Metropolitan Police in 1900.

SARACENS HEAD INN

92 Saracens Head Yard, EC3

A famous tavern and coaching inn. Demolished during the construction of the Holborn viaduct.

SCOTLAND YARD

Whitehall Place, SW1

Derives its name from a palace which

SERJEANTS' INN

5 Chancery Lane, WC2

Originally the seat of the Honourable Society of Judges and Serjeants-at-Law.

SHEPHERD'S MARKET

7 Shepherd Street, W1

Established by Edward Shepherd in

In 1735 Edward Shepherd Esq. obtained His Majesty's Grant from George II for a market place to be sited where the May Fair had been celebrated since c.1532, and it was to this area that the hungry and weary traveller would repair for rest and sustenance.

1735 on the site of the ancient May Fair.

STANDARD IN CORNHILL

Corner of Cornhill and Gracechurch Street, EC3

Built by a German, Peter Morris, it supplied water from the Thames, conveyed by lead pipes, to the adjoining zone until 1603. It was used afterwards as a measurement point from the city to suburban areas.

STOCKS MARKET

Mansion House, EC4

On the site now occupied by the Mansion House stood a meat and fish market founded by Henry Walis, a former lord mayor, until its destruction during the Great Fire. It was rebuilt and converted to a fruit and vegetable market, subsequently transferred to Farringdon Street.

STRYPE STREET

10 Leyden Street, E1

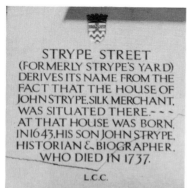

Derived its name from the two Strypes, father and son, who lived here. John Strype the elder was a prosperous silk merchant of Flemish descent. John Strype the younger (1643–1737) was a prolific historian and biographer, author of *Memorials of Cranmer* (1694) and *Annals of the Reformation* (1709–31).

SUNDAY TIMES

4 Salisbury Court, EC4

The first number of the *Sunday Times* was edited here in October 1822.

TOYNBEE HALL

Toynbee Hall, Commercial Street, E1

Founded to the memory of Arnold

Toynbee (1852–83), historian and social reformer, professor of economics and economic history at Balliol College, Oxford, and author of *The Industrial Revolution in England* published posthumously in 1884.

WORLD WAR ONE

Bedford Hotel, Southampton Row, WC1

Site of where one of the first bombs fell on London, September 1917.

WORLD WAR TWO

Railway Bridge, Grover Road, Bow, E1

Site of where the first flying bomb fell, June 1944.

INDEX OF PEOPLE

Names in **bold type** are people commemorated with a blue plaque.

Abbas, Ali Mohamed, 11
Aberdeen, Lord, 114
Adam, James, 186
Adam, Robert, 186
Adams, C.F., 11
Adams, Henry Brooks, 11
Adams, John, 11
Addison, Joseph, 120
Adelaide of Saxe-Meiningen, 34
Agoult, Comtesse d', 90
Ainsworth, Harrison, 39
Albemarle, Duke of, 137
Alexander, George, 117
Allenby, Edmund Henry Hynman, 1st Viscount, 12
Amherst, General, 160
Amundsen, Roald, 133
Anderson, Elizabeth Garrett, 12, 51
Anne, Princess, 182
Anne, Queen of England, 109
Arbuthnot, John, 120
Arthur, Prince, 28
Asquith, Herbert Henry, 1st Earl of Oxford and Asquith, 12–13, 83, 91
Attlee, Clement Richard, 1st Earl Attlee, 13
Auchinleck, Lord, 22
Austen, Jane, 13

Baden-Powell, Agnes, 14
Baden-Powell, Robert Stephenson Smyth, 1st Baron, 14
Bagehot, Walter, 14
Baird, John Logie, 14–15
Bakewell, Thomas, 171
Baldwin, Stanley, 1st Earl Baldwin of Bewdley, 15

Ball, Sir Robert, 46
Ballantyne, Robert Michael, 15
Barbosa, Ruy, 15–16
Baring, Sir Francis, 16
Barnard, Sarah, 51
Barnardo, Thomas John, 16, 99
Barnett, Dame Henrietta, 16
Barnett, Canon Samuel, 16
Barry, Sir Charles, 17
Basire, James, 20
Bathe, Hugo de, 86
Bazalgette, Sir Joseph William, 17
Beauclerk, Charles, 64
Beaufort, 5th Duke, 122
Beaufort, Duke of, 57
Beaufort, Sir Francis, 17–18
Beaumont, George, 37
Bedford, Dukes of, 172
Bedford, 6th Duke, 129
Beecham, Joseph, 18
Beecham, Sir Thomas, 18
Bell, Clive, 171
Bell, Dr Joseph, 44
Ben-Gurion, David, 18–19
Benes, Edvard, 18, 98
Bennett, (Enoch) Arnold, 19
Bentham, Jeremy, 119
Berlioz, Hector, 19
Besant, Annie, 20, 178
Besant, Frank, 20
Bevan, Aneurin, 57
Bicknell, Mary, 37
Blair, Eric Arthur (George Orwell), 113
Blake, William, 20
Blavatsky, Madame, 20
Blemond, Earl of, 172
Bligh, William, 21

Blogg, Frances, 31
Bloomfield, Robert, 21
Bloomsbury Group, 82, 161, 171
Boleyn, Anne, 29, 105, 188
Bolivar, Simon, 21-2
Bollein, Geoffrey, 188
Bonaparte, Louis, 107
Bonaparte, Napoleon *see* **Napoleon, Charles Louis Napoleon Bonaparte**
Bonaparte, Napoleon *see* Napoleon I
Booth, Alfred, 22
Booth, Barton, 170
Booth, Charles, 22
Boswell, James, 22-3, 79, 183
Boucher, Catherine, 20
Bouvier, Jacqueline Lee, 82
Bowers, Lt, 133
Brandt, Carolina, 154
Brawne, Fanny, 81
Braybrooke, Lord, 117
Breuer, Josef, 55
Bridges, Robert, 72
Bright, John, 169
Bright, Richard, 23
Brooke, Sir Charles, 23
Brooke, James, 23
Brougham, Lord, 175
Bruckner, Anton, 23
Brummell, George Bryan (Beau), 23-4
Brunel, Isambard Kingdom, 181
Brunel, Sir Marc Isambard, 181
Buckhurst, Lord, 64
Buckingham, George Villiers, 2nd Duke, 24-5
Buckland, William, 91
Bunning, J.B., 175
Burbage, James, 178, 188
Burbage, Richard, 178
Burgoyne, John, 25
Burke, Edmund, 25, 27, 54
Burlington, Earl of, 26
Burne-Jones, Edward, 105, 128-9
Burr, Margaret, 57
Byron, Lord George Gordon, 50, 135

Campbell, Colen, 26
Campbell, Mrs Patrick, 117
Campbell-Bannerman, Sir Henry, 13
Canaletto (Canal, Antonio), 26

Canning, George, 26-7
Canning, Stratford, 26
Careton, Lord, 25
Carlisle, Earl of, 148
Carlyle, Thomas, 27-8
Caroline, Queen of England, 38
Casement, Sir Roger, 122
Caslon, William, 28
Castlereagh, Lord, 27, 100
Catharine, of Aragon, 28-9, 105
Cavendish, Charles, 29
Cavendish, Henry, 29
Cayley, Sir George, 29
Chain, Ernst, 53
Challoner, Richard, 29-30
Chamberlain, (Arthur) Neville, 30, 33
Chamberlain, Joseph, 30
Chancellor, Richard, 159
Chaplin, Charles Spencer, 30
Chaplin, Charlie, 175
Charcot, Jean Martin, 55
Charles I, 24, 149
Charles II, 25, 64, 116, 149, 186
Charlotte, Queen of England, 57, 75, 106
Chatterton, Thomas, 30-1, 94
Chaucer, Geoffrey, 169
Chenu, Pierre Francois, 93
Chesterton, Gilbert Keith, 31-2
Chopin, Frederic, 32
Christian, Fletcher, 21
Churchill, Lord Randolph Henry Spencer, 32-3
Churchill, Sir Winston Leonard Spencer, 13, 30, 33
Clairmont, Claire, 135
Clarence, Duke of, 33-4
Clemens, Samuel Langhorne ('Mark Twain'), 146
Clive, Robert, 34
Cobden, Richard, 169
Cobden-Sanderson, Thomas James, 34
Cockerell, Samuel Pepys, 190
Cole, Sir Henry, 34
Coleridge, Samuel Taylor, 35-6, 85, 174
Coleridge-Taylor, Samuel, 36
Colet, Dr John, 191
Collins, Sam, 175
Collinson, Peter, 36
Colt, June, 104

Conrad, Joseph, 36–7
Constable, John, 37
Cook, James, 21, 37–8
Cornwall, 1st Duke (Black Prince), 180
Cranmer, Archbishop, 29
Cromwell, Oliver, 45, 96, 145, 149
Crookes, Sir William, 38
Crosby, Sir John, 176
Cross, John, 48
Cruden, Alexander, 38
Cruikshank, George, 38–9
Cruikshank, Isaac, 39
Curtis, William, 39

Dance, George, the elder, 40
Dance, George, the younger, 40
Dandré, Victor, 116
Darwin, Charles, 40–1, 52, 76, 91
Davenant, Sir William, 45
Davies, Ivor Novello ('Ivor Novello'), 111
Davies, Tom, 22
Davy, Humphry, 51
Day, John, 169
De Gaulle, Charles André Joseph Marie, 41–2
De Quincy, Thomas, 72
Defoe, Daniel, 41
Derby, Lord, 25, 43
Devendranath, Maharshi, 142
Devereaux, Robert, Earl of Essex, 178
Devonshire, Duke of, 27
Diaghilev, Sergei Pavlovich, 82
Dickens, Charles, 39, 42–3, 74, 178
Dickinson, G. Lowes, 54
Disraeli, Benjamin, 1st Earl of Beaconsfield, 43, 60
Dodsley, Robert, 25
Doesburg, Theo van, 104
Douglas (George) Norman, 43
Douglas, Lord Alfred, 158
Dowson, Ernest Christopher, 43–4
Doyle, Sir Arthur Conan, 44–5
Doyle, Richard, 44
Dryden, John, 45
Du Maurier, George Louis Palmella Busson, 45
Dugdale, Florence, 66
Duran, Carolus, 132
Durham, Lord, 151

Dutton, William, 96

Earnshaw, Thomas, 46
Eastlake, Sir Charles Lock, 46
Eddington, Sir Arthur Stanley, 46
Edgar, King of England, 193
Edison, Thomas, 56
Edward VI, 174, 178, 187
Edward VII, 86
Edward VIII, 15
Edwardes, William, 2nd Lord Kensington, 177
Edwards, Edward, 46–7
Einstein, Albert, 50
Eisenhower, Dwight David, 47
Elgar, Sir Edward, 47–8
Elgin, Lord, 88
'Eliot, George' (Mary Ann Evans), 48
Eliot, Thomas Stearns, 49, 50
Elizabeth I, 104, 169, 178, 180
Ellis, Henry Havelock, 49
Engels, Friedrich, 49–50, 97
Epstein, Sir Jacob, 50
Essex, Earl of, 190
Eugénie, ex-Empress, 107
Evans, Petty Officer, 133
Evans, Mary Ann ('George Eliot'), 48
Ewart, William, 50

Fairfax, Lord, 25, 96
Faisal, Emir, 89
Faraday, Michael, 51
Fawcett, Henry, 51
Fawcett, Dame Millicent, 12, 51
Fawcett, Philippe, 51
Fielding, Henry, 172
Fisher, Archdeacon, 37
Fitzgerald, Edward, 144
Fitzroy, Robert, 52
Fitzwarin, Alice, 156
Fitzwarin, Sir Ivo, 156
Flaxman, John, 20, 52
Flecker, James Elroy, 52
Fleming, Sir Alexander, 52–3
Fleming, Sir John Ambrose, 53
Flinders, Sir Matthew, 53
Florey, Sir Howard, 53
Forster, Edward Morgan, 53–4, 171
Fox, Charles James, 27, 54–5
Franklin, Benjamin, 55

Franklin, James, 55
Frederick, Prince of Wales, 118
Freud, Sigmund, 55–6, 80
Fricker, Edith, 35
Fricker, Sara, 35
Friese-Greene, William, 56
Froude, Richard Hurrel, 108
Fry, Elizabeth, 56
Fry, Joseph, 56
Furnival, Sir William, 178

Gainsborough, Thomas, 57
Gaitskell, Hugh Todd Naylor, 57
Galton, Sir Francis, 57–8
Gandhi, Mohandas Karamchand, 58–9
Garrick, David, 111, 136
Gaudier-Brzeska, Henri, 59
Gauguin, Paul, 150
Gay, John, 120
George I, 65, 137
George II, 173
George III, 33, 57, 67, 75, 106, 110, 118, 165, 191
George IV, 24, 34, 100
Gibbon, Edward, 59–60
Gibbons, Grinling, 172
Giffird, Emma, 66
Gillman, James, 35–6
Gladstone, Ethel, 92
Gladstone, William Ewart, 60, 124, 126–7
Glaisher, James, 60–1
Godwin, Edward, 143
Godwin, George, 61
Godwin, Mary, 135, 191
Godwin, William, 85, 134–5
Goethe, Johann, 27
Goldsmith, Oliver, 22, 111, 183
Gonne, Maud, 163
Gordon, General, 83
Gosse, Sir Edmund William, 61
Gosse, Philip Henry, 61
Gottwald, Klements, 18
Gounod, Charles Francois, 61
Grace, William Gilbert, 61–2
Graham, George, 145
Grahame, Kenneth, 62
Gravelot, Hubert, 57
Gray, Thomas, 62
Green, John Richard, 63

Green, Joseph Henry, 136
Gregory, Lady, 163
Grey, Earl, 114, 129
Grey, Earl de, 124
Grey, Edward, Viscount Grey of Falloden, 63
Grey, Thomas, 153
Grote, George, 63
Gwynne, Nell, 64
Gwynne, Sarah, 156

Haldane, Richard Burdon, 1st Viscount, 65
Halley, Edmond, 192
Hambleden, Viscountess, 137
Hamilton, Lady Emma, 108, 126
Hamilton, Sir William, 108
Handel, George Frederick, 65
Hansom, Joseph Aloysius, 65–6
Hanson, Joshua Flesher, 172
Hardy, Harriet, 101
Hardy, Thomas, 66
Harmsworth, Alfred Charles William, 1st Viscount Northcliffe, 66–7
Harrison, John, 67
Hart, Emma, 126
Harte, Francis Bret, 67–8
Harvey, William, 170
Hastings, Warren, 136
Hawkins, Sir Anthony Hope ('Anthony Hope'), 68
Hawksmoor, Nicholas, 191
Hawthorne, Nathaniel, 68–9
Haydn, Franz, 75
Hayman, Francis, 57
Hazlitt, William, 69, 72, 81
Heine, Heinrich, 69–70
Henderson, Arthur, 70
Henry I, 170
Henry II, 131
Henry III, 179
Henry IV, 156
Henry V, 156
Henry VII, 28
Henry VIII, 28–9, 105, 179, 185, 186
Henslow, John Stevens, 40
Herbert, Lady Mary, 74
Herzen, Alexander, 70

Heseltine, Philip Arnold ('Peter Warlock'), 153
Hicks, John, 66
Hill, Sir Rowland, 70–1
Hitler, Adolf, 91
Hobbs, Sir John (Jack) Berry, 71
Hodgkin, Thomas, 71
Hoes, Hannah, 148
Hogarth, Catherine, 42
Hogarth, William, 71, 187
Hogg, Quintin, 71
Hogg, Thomas Jefferson, 134
Holland, 1st Lord, 54
Home, Anne, 75
Hood, Lord, 108
Hood, Thomas, 72
'Hope, Anthony' (Sir Anthony Hope Hawkins), 68
Hopkins, Gerard Manley, 72
Hore-Belisha, 1st Baron, 72–3
Howard, Lady Elizabeth, 45
Hudson, Thomas, 123
Hudson, William Henry, 73
Hügel, Baron Friedrich von, 73–4
Hunt, Holman, 101, 128
Hunt, James Henry Leigh, 69, 74, 81, 135, 162, 174
Hunter, John, 75
Hunter, William, 75
Huntingdon, Earl of, 148
Hutchinson, Sir Jonathan, 75–6
Huxley, Sir Julian Sorell, 76, 155
Huxley, Thomas Henry, 76

Irving, Sir Henry, 140, 143
Irving, Washington, 77
Isaacs, Rufus Daniel, 122–3

Jackson, Andrew, 148
James I, 185
James, Henry, 78
James, William, 78
Jefferies, John Richard, 78
Jellicoe, John Rushworth, 1st Earl, 78–9
Jerome, Jeanette, 32
Jinnah, Mohammed Ali, 79
Johnson, Dr Samuel, 22–3, 79–80, 94, 111, 174, 183
Jones, Ernest, 80

Jonson, Ben, 183
Jordan, Mrs, 34
Juliana, Queen of the Netherlands, 158
Jung, C.G., 56

Karno, Fred, 30
Karsavina, Tamara, 81
Kaunitz, Countess Eleonore von, 100
Keats, John, 31, 74, 81
Keith, Sir William, 55
Kelvin, Lord, 93
Kemnie, Charles, 154
Kennedy, John Fitzgerald, 81–2
Kennedy, Joseph, 160
Kenneth, King of Scotland, 193
Keppel, Commodore, 123
Keynes, John Maynard, 82
Kipling, Rudyard, 82–3
Kitchener, Horatio Herbert, 1st Earl, 83
Knoblock, Edward, 19
Knox, Edmund George Valpy, 83–4
Kokoshka, Oskar, 84
Kossuth, Louis, 84

Lamb, Charles, 69, 72, 81, 85–6, 174
Lamb, Mary, 85–6
Lang, Andrew, 86
Langtry, Edward, 86
Langtry, Lillie, 86
Laski, Harold Joseph, 86–7
Lauder, Sir Harry, 87, 175
Law, Andrew Bonar, 15
Lawrence, David Herbert, 87
Lawrence, John Laird Mair, 1st Baron, 87–8
Lawrence, Thomas Edward, 88–9
Lecky, William Edward Hartpole, 89
Leigh Hunt *see* Hunt, James Henry Leigh
Leighton, Frederic, 1st Baron, 89
Lengdon, Olivia, 146
Lenin, Vladimir Ilyich, 89–90
Lewes, George Henry, 48
Lewis, Mary Anne, 43
Lewis, Wyndham, 59
Linacre, Thomas, 186
Linley, Elizabeth, 136
Linnaeus, Carolus, 39
Lister, Joseph, 1st Baron Lister of Lyme Regis, 90

Liszt, Franz, 90
Lloyd, Edward, 182
Lloyd-George, David, 1st Earl of Dwyfor, 33, 90-1, 102
Longfellow, Henry Wadsworth, 36
Lopez-Pumarejo, Alfonso, 91
Lopokova, Lydia, 82
Lord, Thomas, 183
Louis XIV, King of France, 129
Lyell, Sir Charles, 91

McArthur, General, 47
Macaulay, Mary, 22
Macaulay, Thomas Babington, 1st Baron, 92
MacDonald, James Ramsay, 13, 92-3, 181
MacDowell, Patrick, 93
McMillan, Margaret, 93
McMillan, Rachel, 93
Malone, Edmond, 94
Manby, Aaron, 94
Manby, Charles, 94
Mansbridge, Albert, 94
'Mansfield, Katherine' (Kathleen Middleton Murry), 94
Manson, Sir Patrick, 95
Marconi, Guglielmo, Marchese, 95
Marlborough, 1st Duke, 148, 170
Marlborough, 7th Duke, 32
Marlborough, Duchess of, 150
Marsden, William, 95
Marvell, Andrew, 96
Marx, Karl Heinrich, 50, 96-7
Mary I, 125
Mary, Queen of Scots, 29
Masaryk, Thomas Garrigue, 18, 97-8
Maskeleyne, Margaret, 34
Maugham, William Somerset, 50, 98-9
Maxim, Sir Hiram Stevens, 99
Mazzini, Guiseppe, 99
Mecklenburg-Schwerin, Henry, Duke of, 158
Melbourne, Lord, 92
Menteith, Sir John, 152
Merchant, Elizabeth, 116
Meredith, George, 99-100
Metternich, Prince Clemens Lothar Wenzel, 100
Middleton, Edward, 17
Mill, James, 100-1

Mill, John Stuart, 100-1, 162
Millais, Sir John Everett, 101, 128
Milner, Alfred, 1st Viscount, 101-2
Milton, John, 96, 102-3, 192
Minshull, Elizabeth, 103
Minto, Lord, 121
Miranda, Francisco de, 103
Mondrian, Piet Cornelis, 103-4
Monmouth, Duke of, 41
Montcalm, Louis Joseph, Marquis de, 160
Montefiore, Sir Moses, 104
Montgomerie, Margaret, 22
Moore, G.E., 54
Morden, John, 104
Mordkin, Mikhail, 116
More, Sir Thomas, 104-5, 176, 181
Morgan, John, 35
Morrell, Lady Ottoline, 105
Morris, Peter, 194
Morris, William, 34, 105, 128
Morrison, Herbert Stanley, Baron Morrison of Lambeth, 105
Morse, Samuel Finley Breese, 105-6
Mozart, Wolfgang Amadeus Chrysostom, 106
Munnings, Sir Alfred, 106
Murry, John Middleton, 94
Murry, Kathleen Middleton ('Katherine Mansfield'), 94

Nabuco, Joaquim, 107
Napoleon, Charles Louis Napoleon Bonaparte, 107
Napoleon I, of France, 100, 107, 138
Napoleon III, of France, 107
Necker, Jacques, 138
Nelson, Horatio, Viscount Nelson, 107-8
Nesbit, Edith, 178
Nesbit, Frances, 108
Newman, John Henry, Cardinal, 108-9
Newman, Robert, 160
Newton, Sir Isaac, 109
Nicolls, Mary Ellen, 100
Nightingale, Florence, 109-10
Nightingale, William, 110
Nollekens, Joseph, 110
North, Lord, 24, 54
Northcliffe, Lord see Harmsworth, Alfred Charles William

Novello, Dame Clara, 111
'Novello, Ivor' (Ivor Novello Davies), 111
Nuddleton, Alice, 104

Oates, Laurence Edward Grace, 112, 133
Obradovich, Dositey, 112
O'Connor, Father, 31
Onslow, Arthur, 113
Orford, 4th Earl, 129
'Orwell, George' (Eric Arthur Blair), 113
Oswald, Lee, 82
Outwich, family, 190
Owen, Robert, 70

Palmer, Samuel, 20
Palmerston, Henry John Temple, 3rd
   Viscount, 114
Parkinson, James, 114
Parry, Sir W.E., 127
Parsons, Sir Charles Algernon, 115
Patel, Sardar Vallabhbhai Javerbhai, 115
Pattle, Eliza Susan, 151
Pavlova, Anna, 115–16
Payne-Townsend, Charlotte, 134
Peabody, George, 116
Peabody, Sophia, 68
Peacock, Thomas Love, 100
Peel, Sir Robert, 60
Pepys, Samuel, 116–17
Percy, Henry (Hotspur), 184
Petrie, Sir William Matthew Flinders, 117
Pickering, Sir Gilbert, 45
Pierce, Franklin, 68
Pinero, Sir Arthur Wing, 117–18
Pitt, William, 1st Earl of Chatham, 93,
   118, 160
Pitt, William, the younger, 27, 54, 93,
   118–19, 139, 157
Pius VI, Pope, 143
Place, Francis, 119
Pombal, Sebastiao Joeś de Carvalho e
   Mello, Marquess of, 119–20
Pope, Alexander, 120, 150
Portland, Duke of, 27
Pound, Ezra, 49, 59
Powell, Mary, 102
Primrose, General James, 125
Pybus, Catherine, 137

Quarles, Francis, 189

Queensberry, Marquess of, 158
Queyney, Richard, 171

Raffles, Sir Thomas Stamford, 121
Raglan, Lady Emily, 122
Raglan, Fitzroy James Henry Somerset,
   1st Baron, 121–2
Rahere, 170, 187
Rammohun Roy, 122
Rathbone, Eleanor, 122
Reading, Rufus Daniel Isaacs, 1st
   Marquess of, 122–3
Reschid Pasha, Mustapha, 123
Reynoids, Sir Joshua, 22, 94, 123
Ricardo, David, 101
Richard II, 171
Richtofen, Frieda von, 87
Ripon, 1st Earl, 123
Ripon, George Frederick Samuel
   Robinson, Marquess of, 123–4
Rizal, José, 124
Robbins, Amy, 155
Roberts, Caroline, 47
Roberts, Frederick Sleigh, Earl Roberts
   of Kandahar, Pretoria, and Waterford,
   124–5
Rogers, John, 125
'Rohmer, Sax' (Arthur Sarsfield Wood),
   125–6
Rokesley, Gregory de, 126
Romney, George, 126
Ronalds, Sir Francis, 126
Rosebery, Archibald Philip Primrose, 5th
   Earl, 126
Rosee, Pasqua, 185
Ross, Sir James Clark, 127
Ross, Sir Ronald, 127–8
Ross, Sir John, 127
Rosse, 3rd Earl, 115
Rossetti, Christina, 128
Rossetti, Dante Gabriel, 101, 105, 128, 162
Rossetti, William Michael, 128
Rowlandson, Thomas, 129
Ruskin, John, 156
Russell, Edward, Earl of Orford, 129
Russell, John, 1st Earl, 129–30
'Rutherford, Mark' (William Hale
   White), 130

St Thomas à Becket, 131, 190

Salisbury, Lord, 32
Salt, Samuel, 85
San Martin, José de, 131
Sand, George, 32
Sandwich, Earl of, 116
Sargent, John Singer, 132
Savarkar, Vinayak Damodar, 132
Scheemakers, Peter, 110
Schiller, Johann, 35
Scott, Robert Falcon, 112, 132–3
Seferis (Seferiades), George, 133
Severn, Charles, 81
Shackleton, Sir Ernest Henry, 133–4
Shakespeare, William, 171, 179, 183
Sharp, Cecil James, 134
Shaw, George Bernard, 20, 50, 134, 178
Shaw, Richard Norman, 193
Shawe, Isabella, 144
Shelley, Percy Bysshe, 31, 74, 81, 134–5, 191
Shepherd, Edward, 193
Sheraton, Thomas, 135
Sheridan, Richard Brinsley, 135–6
Shrewsbury, Earl of, 25
Siddal, Elizabeth, 128
Siddons, Sarah, 57
Simon, Sir John, 136
Sloane, Sir Hans, 1st Baronet, 136–7, 179
Smith, Adam, 101
Smith, Frederick Edwin, 1st Earl of Birkenhead, 137
Smith, John, 117
Smith, Joseph, 26
Smith, Sydney, 137–8
Smith, William Henry, 137
Smithson, Harriet, 19
Smollett, Tobias, 174
Southey, Robert, 31, 35
Spencer, Herbert, 48
Stanhope, Charles, 3rd Earl, 138–9
Staël, Anne Louise Germaine Necker, Madame de, 138
Staël-Holstein, Baron de, 138
Stephen, Sir Leslie, 161
Stephenson, George, 139, 145
Stephenson, Robert, 139
Sterne, Laurence, 111, 129
Stoker, Abraham (Bram), 139–40
Strachey, Lytton, 171

Strang, William, 140
Strype, John, the elder, 194–5
Strype, John, the younger, 194–5
Stuart, John McDouall, 140
Suess, Eduard, 140
Sun Yat-Sen (Sun Wen), 140–1
Swift, Jonathan, 120
Syme, Agnes, 90
Syme, James, 90
Symons, George James, 141
Szabo, Etienne, 141
Szabo, Violette, 141

Tagore, Prince Dwarkaneth, 142
Tagore, Sir Rabindranath, 142
Talleyrand-Périgord, Charles Maurice de, 100, 138, 142–3
Talleyrand-Périgord, Lt General Charles Maurice de, 142
Tennant, Margot, 13
Tennyson, Alfred, Lord, 144, 162
Terry, Dame Ellen Alice, 143
Thackeray, William Makepeace, 45, 143–4, 174
Theobald, Archbishop of Canterbury, 131
Thomas à Becket *see* **St Thomas à Becket**
Thomson, Elspeth, 62
Thornhill, Sir James, 71
Thornycroft, Thomas, 144
Thornycroft, Sir William Hamo, 144
Thurloe, John, 96, 144–5
Tompion, Thomas, 145
Tourville, Anne Hilarion de Cotentin, Comte de, 129
Townley, Charles, 145
Toynbee, Arnold, 195
Trevelyan, G.M., 54
Trevithick, Richard, 145
Turner, Ellen, 151
Turner, Joseph Mallord William, 145–6
'Twain, Mark' (Samuel Langhorne Clemens), 146
Tyler, Wat, 169
Tyrwhitt, Thomas, 31

Unwin, Sir Stanley, 147

Van Buren, Martin, 148–9
Van Gogh, Theo, 149–50

Van Gogh, Vincent Willem, 149
Vanbrugh, Sir John, 148
Vane, Sir Henry, 149
Velazquez, Diego Rodriguez de Silva y, 132
Victoria, Queen of England, 34, 43, 89, 107
Vogler, Abt, 154
Voltaire (Francois Marie Arouet de), 149
Vulliamy, Marie, 100

Wagner, Richard, 90
Wakefield, Edward Gibbon, 151
Walis, Henry, 194
Wallace, Edgar, 151–2
Wallace, Sir William, 152
Wallis, Henry, 100
Walpole, Horace, 4th Earl of Orford, 62, 94, 153
Walpole, Sir Robert, 1st Earl of Orford, 118, 152–3
Walter, John, 153
Ward, Arthur Sarsfield ('Sax Rohmer'), 125–6
Wardell, E.A., 143
'Warlock, Peter' (Philip Arnold Heseltine), 153
Washington, George, 103
Watts, G.F., 143
Waugh, Benjamin, 153–4
Webb, Beatrice, 178
Webb, Philip, 105
Webb, Sidney, 178
Weber, Carl Maria Friedrich Ernst von, 154
Weizmann, Chaim, 154–5
Wellcome, Lady, 98–9
Wellesley, Sir Arthur, Duke of Wellington, 122, 123, 172
Wells, G.P., 155
Wells, Herbert George, 155
Wells, Isabel, 155
Welsh, Jane Baillie, 27–8
Wesley, Charles, 155–6, 180
Wesley, John, 155
Westbrook, Harriet, 134

Westphalen, Jenny von, 96
Whistler, James Abbott McNeil, 156
Whitbread, Samuel, 156
White, William Hale ('Mark Rutherford'), 130
Whittington, Sir Richard, 156–7, 184
Wilberforce, William, 157, 175
Wilde, Oscar Fingall O'Flahertie Wills, 86, 157–8
Wilhelm III, King of the Netherlands, 158
Wilhelmina, Helena Pauline Maria of Orange-Nassau, Queen of the Netherlands, 158
Willan, Dr Robert, 158
William I (the Conqueror), 172, 190
William III, 41, 182
William IV, 33–4
William of Wykeham, 190
Willoughby, Sir Hugh, 158–9
Wilson, Edward Adrian, 133, 159
Wilson, President, 98
Wilson, Sir James, 14
Winant, John Gilbert, 159–60
Wingfield, Major Walter Clopton, 160
Wolfe, General Edward, 160
Wolfe, James, 160
Wood, Sir Henry Joseph, 160–1
Woodcock, Catherine, 103
Woolf, Leonard Sidney, 161
Woolf, Virginia, 161, 171
Woolner, Thomas, 161–2
Wordsworth, William, 31, 35
Wren, Sir Christopher, 162, 187, 188, 191, 192
Wycherley, William, 120, 172

Yarborough, Henrietta Maria, 148
Yeats, Jack, 163
Yeats, John Butler, 163
Yeats, William Butler, 163–4
Young, Thomas, 163

Zoffany, Johann, 165

INDEX OF
HISTORICAL SITES

Aldersgate, 169
Aldgate, 169
Anti-Corn-Law Offices, 169

Barton Street, 170
Bell Inn, 170–1
Bethlehem Hospital (second), 171
Blackheath Hall, 171
Blackwell Hall, 171
Bow Street (19–20), WC2, 172
Bull Inn, 172

Campden Hill Square, W11, 172
Cato Street Conspiracy, 172–3
Chelsea China, 173–4
Chelsea Physic Garden, 174
Cheshire Cheese, 174
Chiswick Square, 174
Christ's Hospital, 174
City of London School, 174–5
Clapham Sect, Holy Trinity Church, 175
Clink Prison, 175
Collins' Music-Hall, 175
Compter, Giltspur Street, 176
Crosby Hall, 176

Davies Amphitheatre, 176
Devil Tavern, 177

Edwardes Square, 177

Fabian Society, 178
French Protestant Church, 178
Furnival's Inn, 178

Globe Theatre, 178–9, 188

Greyfriars Monastery, 179

Henry VIII's Manor House, 179
Hippodrome Race Course, 179

John Bray's House, 180
Joiners and Ceilers Company, 180

Kennington Palace, 180–1

Labour Party House, 181
Lindsey House, 181
Lloyd's Coffee House, 182
London House, 182
Lords Cricket Ground, 183
Loriners' Hall, 183

May Fair, 183, 194
Mitre Tavern, 183
Moor Gate, 183–4

Newgate, 184
Northumberland House, 184

Orange Street Congregational Church, 184

Parish Clerks' Company, 184–5
Pasqua Rosee's Head, 185
Peterborough Court, 185
Post House Yard, 185–6
Poulters' Hall, 185

Rosebank, 186
Royal College of Physicians, 186
Royal Society for the Encouragement of Arts
    Manufacturers and Commerce, 186

St Andrew Hubbard, 186
St Augustine Papey, 186–7
St Bartholomew the Great, 187
St Bartholomew's Hospital, 152, 170
St Benet Gracechurch, 187
St Dunstan, 187–8
St Gabriel, 188
St John the Baptist (Priory of), 188
St John the Evangelist, 188
St Lawrence Jewry, 188
St Leonard Eastcheap, 189
St Leonard's, 189
St Martin, 190
St Martin Outwich, 190
St Mary Cole, 190
St Mary Woolchurch Haw, 191
St Mary-Le-Bow, 190

St Michael Bassishaw, 191
St Mildred's Church, 191
St Paul's School, 191–2
St Stephen Walbrook, 192
Saracens Head Inn, 193
Scotland Yard, 193
Serjeant's Inn, 193
Shepherd's Market, 193–4
Standard in Cornhill, 194
Stocks Market, 194
Strype Street, 194–5
Sunday Times, 195

Toynbee Hall, 195

World War One, 195
World War Two, 195

INDEX OF
STREETS

Adam Street, WC2, 151, 186
Addison Bridge Place, W14, 35, 86
Addison Road, W14
Albert Bridge Road, SW11, 43
Albion Street, W2, 23
Aldersgate Street, EC1, 95, 169, 178, 182, 184
Aldgate Street, EC3, 169
Aldorf Street, W1, 159
Aldridge Villas, W11, 115
Aldwych, WC2, 111
Alexander Square, SW7, 61
Amwell Street, EC1, 38
Archery Road, SE9, 105
Argyll Street, W1, 77, 138
Arlington Street, SW1, 152
Avonmore Road, W14, 47

Baker Street, W1, 19, 118
Bankside, SE1, 28, 162
Barton Street, SW1, 88
Barton Street, W1, 170
Basinghall Street, EC2, 191
Bayham Street, NW1, 42
Beak Street, W1, 26
Bear Garden Street, E1, 176
Beaumont Street, W1, 63
Bedford Square, WC1, 29, 68, 71, 122
Bell Inn Yard, EC3, 170
Belmont Grove, SE13, 43
Ben Jonson Road, E1, 16
Bennett Park, SE3, 46
Bentinck Street, W1, 59
Berkeley Square, W1, 26, 34
Bishopgate Street, EC2, 172
Blackheath, SE10, 171

Blandford Street, W1, 51
Bloomsbury Place, WC1, 136
Bloomsbury Square, WC1, 158, 171
Bouverie Street, EC4, 69
Brompton Square, SW3, 119
Brook Street, W1, 26, 65
Brooke Street, SW3, 30
Broomwood Road, SW11, 157
Bryanston Square, W1, 123
Buckingham Street, WC2, 117
Burnley Road, SW9, 141

Cadogan Place, SW1, 157
Cadogan Square, SW1, 19
Camden Passage, N1, 38
Camden Square, NW1, 141
Campden Hill Square, W8, 140
Campden Hill, W8, 92
Cannon Place, NW3, 117
Canonbury Square, N1, 113
Canterbury Crescent, SW9, 49
Cardinal's Wharf, Bankside, SE1, 28, 162
Carlton Gardens, SW1, 41, 83
Cato Street, W1, 172
Cavendish Square, W1, 12, 71, 75, 127
Chalcot Crescent, NW1, 124
Chancery Lane, WC2, 144, 193
Charles Street, W1, 33, 126
Cheapside, EC2, 131, 190
Chelsea Embankment, SW3, 123
Chelsea Park Gardens, SW3, 106
Chepstow Villas, W11, 84
Chesham Place, SW1, 129
Chester Square, SW1, 158
Chesterfield Street, W1, 23, 98

Cheyne Row, SW3, 27
Cheyne Walk, SW3, 28, 48, 104, 145, 156,
    174, 179, 181
Chiswell Street, EC1, 28, 156
Chiswick Square, W4, 174
Clapham Common, SW4, 17, 153, 175
Clarges Street, W1, 54
Clements Lane, EC4, 112
Cleveland Street, W1, 105
Clifton Gardens, W9, 53
Clink Street, SE1, 175
Cloth Fair, EC1, 187
Colby Road, SE19, 20
College Hill, EC4, 24, 156
Commercial Street, E1, 195
Connaught Place, W2, 32
Cornhill, EC3, 62, 194
Cornwall Gardens, SW7, 107
Craven Street, WC2, 55, 69
Crescent Wood Road, SE26, 14
The Crest, NW4, 104
Cromms Hill, SE10, 153
Cromwell Avenue, N6, 132
Crown Office Row, EC4, 85
Curtain Road, EC2, 188
Curzon Street, W1, 122

Dagnall Park, SE25, 36
Danvers Street, SW3, 52
Dartmouth Hill, EC4, 60
De Vere Gardens, W8, 78
Dean Street, W1, 96
Devonshire Street, W1, 117
Dorset Square, NW1, 183
Draycott Place, SW3, 78
Duke Street, W1, 21
Duncan Terrace, N1, 86, 140

Earls Terrace, W8, 177
East Heath Road, NW3, 94
Eastcheap, EC3, 186, 189
Eaton Place, SW1, 50
Eaton Square, SW1, 15, 30, 100, 116
Ebury Street, SW1, 106
Eccleston Square, SW1, 33
Eglinton Road School, SE18, 60
Eliot Place, SE3, 127
Elm Row, NW3, 34
Elsworthy Road, NW3, 160

Enfield Town Station, 81
Englewood Road, SW12, 71
Essex Street, WC2, 178

Farringdon Street, EC4, 181, 194
Fenchurch Street, EC3, 188
Finchley Road, NW8, 84
Finsbury Square, EC2, 23
Fitzroy Road, NW1, 163
Fitzroy Square, W1, 46, 134, 161
Fitzroy Street, W1, 53
Fleet Street, EC4, 79, 145, 151, 174, 177,
    183, 185
Footscray Road, 78
Foster Lane, EC2, 189
Frith Street, W1, 69
Frognal, NW3, 81, 83
Frognal Gardens, NW3, 57
Fulham Road, SW6, 59

George Lane, Heather Green, SE13, 93
Gerrard Street, W1, 25, 45
Gillingham Street, SW1, 36
Gilmore Road, SE13, 52
Giltspur Street, EC1, 176
Gloucester Square, W2, 139
Golden Square, W1, 75, 119
Gordon Square, WC1, 82
Gower Street, WC1, 40, 51, 105, 145
Gracechurch Street, EC3, 39, 187, 194
Grafton Way, W1, 103
Gray's Inn Place, WC1, 140
Great Marlborough Street, W1, 90
Great Portland Street, W1, 22, 154
Great Russell Street, 113
Great Windmill Street, 75
Greenwell Street, W1, 52
Greenwich Park, SE10, 160
Grenville Place, SW7, 22
Gresham Street, EC2, 188
Grosvenor Gardens, SW1, 137
Grosvenor Square, W1, 11, 47
Grove End Road, NW8, 18
Grover Road, Bow, E1, 195
Guildford Street, WC1, 115
Guildhall Yard, EC2, 171
Gwendolen Avenue, SW15, 18

Hackford Road, SW9, 149

Hallam Street, W1, 128
Hamilton Terrace, NW8, 17, 140
Hampstead Grove, NW3, 45
Handen Road, Heather Green, SE2, 147
Hanover Square, W1, 142
Hanover Terrace, NW1, 155
Hans Place, SW1, 13
Harley Street, W1, 91
Hatton Garden, EC1, 99
Hereford Road, W2, 95
Herne Hill, SE24, 125
Hertford Street, W1, 25, 29, 135
High Holborn, EC2, 178
High Holborn, WC1, 46
High Street, N14, 87
Highgate High Street, N6, 96
Hogarth Lane, W4, 71
Holbury Street, SW10, 99
Holford Road, NW3, 73
Holland Park Gardens, W14, 15
Holland Park Road, W14, 89
Holles Street, 50
Holly Bush Hill, NW3, 126
Howitt Road, NW3, 92
Hoxton Square, N1 114
Hyde Park Gate, SW7, 14, 33, 50
Hyde Park Street, W2, 137

Idol Lane, EC3, 46
Islington Green, N1, 175

Jermyn Street, SW1, 109
John Adam Street, WC2, 129
John Street, WC1, 137

Keats Grove, NW3, 81
Kennington Road, SE11, 30
Kennington Road, SE1, 180
Kensington Court Gardens, W8, 49
Kensington Park Gardens, W11, 38
Kensington Square, W8, 100, 136
King Edward Memorial Park, E1, 158
King Edward Street, EC1, 185
King Street, WC2, 129
King's Cross Road, WC1, 89
King's Road, SW3, 143

Ladbroke Grove, W11, 179
Lambeth Road, SE1, 21, 171

Lancaster Gate, W2, 67
Langham Street, W1, 94
Lawford Road, NW5, 113
Lawrence Street, SW3, 173
Laystall Street, EC1, 99
Leicester Square, WC2, 123
Leyden Street, E1, 194
Lincoln's Inn Fields, WC2, 95
Little Britain, EC1, 180
Lombard Street, EC3, 120, 126, 182
London Wall, EC2, 171, 183
Long Acre, WC2, 15
Longley Road, SW17, 87
Ludgate Circus, EC4, 151

Maida Vale, W9, 56
Maiden Lane, WC2, 149
Manchester Square, W1, 101
Manchester Street, W1, 17
Mansfield Street, W1, 138
Mansion House, EC4, 194
Maresfield Gardens, NW3, 55, 134
Marlborough Place, NW8, 76
Marloes Road, W8, 86
Marshall Street, W1, 20
Maze Hill, SE10, 148
Melbury Road, W14, 144
Mile End Road, E1, 37
Milk Street, EC2, 174
Mill Hill, NW7, 36, 121, 186
Monkhams Avenue, Redbridge, 13
Moorfields, 171
Moorgate, EC2, 183
Morden Road, SE3, 61
Mortimer Street, W1, 110
Mortimer Road, N1, 61
Mottingham Lane, SE12, 61
Mount Park Road, South Harrow, 15

Netherhall Gardens, NW3, 48
New Bond Street, W1, 107
Newark Street, E1, 63
Newgate Street, EC1, 174, 179, 184, 191
North End Road, NW11, 115

Oakley Street, SW3, 132
Old Broad Street, EC2, 108
Old Gloucester Street, WC1, 30
Old Jewry, EC2, 190

Old Road, SE13, 16
Onslow Gardens, SW7, 89
Onslow Square, SW7, 52
Orange Street, WC2, 184
Orme Square, W2, 70
Orsett Terrace, W2, 70
Osnaburgh Street, NW1, 178

Palace Gate, W8, 101
Pall Mall, SW1, 57, 64, 186
Pandora Road, NW6, 66
Paradise Road, Richmond, 161
Park Crescent, NW1, 90
Park Hill, Carshalton, 130
Park Lane, W1, 104
Park Road, W8, 131
Park Street, SE1, 178
Parkhill Road, NW3, 103
Phillimore Place, W8, 62
Piccadilly, W1, 114
Platts Lane, NW3, 97
Poland Street, W1, 134
Pond Road, SE3, 68
Pond Street, NW3, 71, 76
Pont Street, SW1, 86
Portland Place, W1, 11, 124
Poultry, EC2, 56, 72, 191
Powis Road, E3, 58
Princes's Gate, SW7, 81

Queen Anne Street, W1, 19, 146
Queen Anne's Gate, SW1, 63, 65, 145

Red House Lane, Bexley Heath, 105
Red Lion Square, WC1, 67, 128
Regent's Park Road, NW1, 49
Rodenhurst Road, SW4, 70
Roehampton, SW15, 72
Rosslyn Hill, NW3, 149
Routh Road, SW18, 90
Russell Road, W14, 79
Russell Street, WC2, 22
Rutland Gate, SW7, 57

St Bartholomew's Hospital, West Smithfield, EC1, 152, 170
St Dunstan Lane, EC3, 187
St George's Square, SW1, 160
St James's Place, SW1, 32

St James's Square, SW1, 118
St Leonard's Terrace, SW3, 139
St Luke's Road, W11, 73
St Martin's-le-Grand, EC1, 185, 190
St Mary Axe, 187
St Mary-le-Bow Church, EC2, 102
St Michael's Alley, EC3, 185
Salisbury Court, EC4, 116, 195
Saracens Head Yard, EC3, 193
Savile Row, W1, 23, 63
Sheffield Terrace, SW1, 32
Shepherd Street, W1, 193
Sloane Avenue, SW3, 133
Smithfield, 176
Soho Square, W1, 113
South Molton Street, W1, 20
South Street, W1, 109
Southampton Row, WC1
Southwark Bridge Road, SE1, 80
Spaniards Road, NW3, 16
Stafford Place, SW1, 72
Stanhope Gate, W1, 121
Stoke Newington Church Street, N16, 41
Strand-on-the-Green, W4, 165
Stratford Place, W1, 148
Sumner Place, SW7, 65
Sussex Square, W2, 33

Tavistock Square, WC1, 11, 42
Tedworth Square, SW3, 146
Telegraph Street, EC2, 21
Tennison Road, SE25, 44
Theobald's Road, WC1, 43
Thornhaugh Street, WC1, 49
Threadneedle Street, EC2, 190
Tite Street, SW3, 132, 153, 157
Trebeck Street, W1, 183
Tressiliant Crescent, SE4, 152
Trinity Road, SW17, 66
Tufton Street, SW1, 122
Turnham Green Terrace, W4, 53

Upper Belgrave Street, SW1, 14
Upper Berkeley Street, W1, 12
Upper Cheyne Row, SW3, 74
Upper Mall, W6, 34, 126
Upper Richmond Road, SW15, 112
Upper Thames Street, EC4, 180

Vale of Health, NW3, 87, 142
Vicarage Crescent, SW11, 159
Villiers Street, WC2, 82

Walbrook Street, EC4, 192
Walbrook, WC4, 191
Wardour Street, W1, 135
Warrington Crescent, W9, 18
Warwick Gardens, W14, 31
Warwick Lane, EC4, 186
Watling Street, EC4, 188
Welbeck Street, W1, 95, 161, 164
Well Walk, NW3, 37
West Smithfield, EC1, 125, 152, 170
Westbourne Terrace, W2, 94

Westwood Hill, SE26, 133
Wetherby Gardens, SW5, 12
Wheatley Street, W1, 155
Whitefriars Street, EC4, 169
Whitehall Place, SW1, 193
Wilton Crescent, SW1, 91
Wimbledon Park Road, SW18, 48
Windsor Road, Ilford, 94
Woburn Walk, WC1, 163
Wood Lane, N6, 93
Wood Street, EC2, 184

York Terrace East, NW1, 80
Young Street, W8, 143